Change Your Life
Through Prayer

Change Your Life Through Prayer

BY
STELLA TERRILL MANN

AUTHOR OF "CHANGE YOUR LIFE THROUGH LOVE"

DeVORSS & CO., *Publishers*
P.O. Box 550
Marina del Rey, CA 90291

Revised and Enlarged

7th Paperback Edition, 1980

ISBN: 0-87516-053-0

Printed in the United States of America
by Book Graphics, Inc., Marina del Rey, California

CONTENTS

DEDICATION

To the readers of my books, students and friends who have joined my perpetual prayer project and who are working with me for a better world through better people, this book is lovingly dedicated.

First printing of the first paper back edition, July, 1971.

Stella Terrill Mann
Pasadena, Calif.

※◆◇◆※

PREFACE

DEAR READER:

This book has come to you. Since nothing can come to you except that which belongs to you or that which you need for your growth, accept it as an answer to a need, and do not let the book go until it gives you a blessing.

Permit me to explain something of its contents and how it came to be written, as an aid to your getting the greatest possible good out of it.

First, let me make it plain that I do not set myself up as an authority or even as a teacher. I am at most only a student of Christianity, but I am so utterly convinced that there is no lasting, no satisfying solution for the problems of the individual or the world, except through Christian principles, that I feel it a duty to share at least as much as I have proved about prayer and applied Christianity as a way of life.

As a child I attended church and Sunday-school, having practically been born in the church. My maternal grandfather moved into the wilds of Arkansas, some fifty miles from a railroad, when my mother was a young girl. Almost before he built a home there, he constructed a crude shack with a thatched roof and held church every Sunday, doing the preaching himself, until he could stir the neighbors into building a proper church with a regularly ordained minister in charge.

Yes, I attended church, but it meant very little to me. When I thought about it at all, it was rather to disagree than agree with what I was taught. I could not accept hell-fire and brimstone, a devil with or without hoofs,

9

tail and pitchfork. Hence, a little learning coupled with considerable doubt, and what, in those days, I thought of loftily as an insult to my intelligence, led me to disregard the whole of it, and rather to agree with my paternal grandfather, who was an original thinker, though he never learned to read or write until after he volunteered for service in the Civil War. He used to say of the old conception of the angry and jealous God who meted out punishment: "He's better than that; I've proved it myself." But as for looking into these matters on my own accord, for my own personal benefit, it never occurred to me. I simply disregarded them.

So I grew up, learning something about Christian principles as a code of ethics, a code of conduct in "how to behave myself," as my mother put it, rather than as a means of solving everyday problems of life. For the instant I was out of my home, I saw a woeful lack of Christian practice in school, in business, in social life, and among some of our best church members; and as I began to take an interest in national and international affairs, I saw that practically nowhere was Christianity practiced.

I gradually came to think of Christianity as an impractical theory, and to think of God much as I had come to think of Santa Claus—wonderful, if only it could be true, but something one could believe in utterly only as a very young child, and something that we should continue to teach the children as a rightful part of childhood. As for prayer, I came to believe that no prayer ever had been answered and that we never could know very much, if anything, about God or the hereafter, nor did I feel any particular need to know.

Later, as my life became bitter, unhappy, and highly complicated with problems I never before knew existed in the world (and I was sure through no fault of my own), it never occurred to me that the solution to them all lay within myself. I still attended church, took my children to Sunday-school, and in a vague way, I often longed for some Being, in Whom I could believe, to Whom I could appeal for help and get a definite answer. That was long before I learned that faith is something like a savings bank; you have to put in before you can draw out, but if you will continue to put in, the interest and compounded interest accruing to you adds up amazingly and surely. But, having put in no faith, I did not try to find God.

My life became more and more complicated, and so filled with problems and unhappiness, that, but for my children, it did not seem worth the living. Then, one day in 1926, between one moment and another, I was suddenly confronted with a situation so terrifying that I knew nothing short of God, a miracle, could save my life. In a flash I learned that prayer is the most powerful force in the universe. For I used it, and not only saved my life in that instant, but subsequently, continuing to use it, healed myself of a condition that was brought about at that terrifying time, which seemed destined to make a cripple of me for life.

After I had recovered from the amazement of my experience, I set to work diligently to learn something about prayer, what it is and how it works. I think my first motive was pure gratitude and a desire to acknowledge a blessing received, and a sense of shame that I did not know surely how to do even that. There followed many failures with prayer. Now and then, I tried prayer as a means for solving a problem and found that it worked. I began to wonder why prayer was not successful every time. I began to see that law was in evidence, here as elsewhere in nature. I determined to learn as much as possible about the laws involving prayer. My first motive has grown into a steady resolve to devote the rest of my life to learning all I can about this power we call prayer, and to sharing my findings with everyone who cares to listen.

I had been forced to read my Bible before. Now I read it eagerly, searchingly. I studied the four gospels, trying to learn the true meaning of Jesus' words, for they began to appear to me as statements of laws, and as such, could be learned and used by anyone. This, of course, is precisely what Jesus said—that anyone could use them.

In my search to learn what others had found out about prayer, I became acquainted with the Unity School of Christianity. I became much interested in their explanations of the meanings of the Bible and of Jesus' words. I was greatly impressed by the many healings and the very practical use that was made of prayer. So my studies increased until I began to be successful in my definite experiments with prayer, and to learn why some efforts were unsuccessful.

Then, taking Jesus' statement that where two or more are gathered together in His name, there would He be also, and that where two could agree on earth concerning a thing, it would be done unto them, I began a series of experiments, working with others and trying to help solve their problems through prayer. I kept account of these experiments.

I do not know what happens, nor why it is, that two, with complete understanding and agreement to a degree which I can best describe as pure knowingness, seem to do more with prayer than one alone, but I have seen it happen too often to doubt it. Hence, in the case histories related here, you will find many references to my insistence on the petitioner's agreement to one point before we went on to another. For in dealing with prayer we are dealing with law no less than we are dealing with laws of mathematics when we add columns of figures.

Along with my Bible studies, I read many works on religion, philosophy, and science. I carried on my individual program of testing by past history the truth or workability of what I considered laws which I found in the Bible, and more especially those in Jesus' teachings. I discovered that not only all recorded history, but every day of our life, every problem with which the world is today confronted, is proof of the truth of the existence of these spiritual laws, and that they are self-operating, never broken. (The examples of proofs are not to be gone into here, but will form the contents of a later book.)

Christian principles as a way of life will yet revolutionize the world. Men will come to them not through the door of formal religion, for men never will agree on religion, but by way of personal experiences in their business and social life. My files are filled with examples of this trend in the business world. Men everywhere are beginning to realize that Jesus spoke pure wisdom and truth, and that as He prayed and got answers, so can we all.

From time to time, since 1934, my experiments with prayer and my general ideas about it have been published by the Unity School of Christianity in their several publications. It was the regular Unity and allied New Thought students who wrote me, from all over the world, of the help they received by trying the experiments I suggested, and the questions they asked for further guidance, that led me to writing a series of articles, "How To Demonstrate," which is a metaphysical term meaning how to solve the problems of life by means of prayer. These articles were published as a series in *Unity Monthly,* starting in December, 1943, and running for nine consecutive months. It was the letters from the general reading public, from people who never before had heard of the

New Thought movement in religion, which led me to revise and greatly enlarge that series of articles into this present work.

This book is really a series of case histories of experiments with prayer, with suggested programs whereby the reader may make his own experiments and change his own life through prayer.

What I have to say here is not the last word on the subject, and maybe not the best word, either. But it is at least a sincere and proven word and is my particular way of helping others solve their problems and change their lives by using the greatest power in the universe—prayer.

In glancing through my case histories one might feel that bringing into reality the desires of the heart by means of prayer is a hit-and-miss gamble. Sometimes the petitioners made their demonstrations, and got their answers. Sometimes they did not. But on careful study of all the facts, the reasons for both failure and success are seen. These are facts which we must here consider, for we learn by failing as well as by succeeding. The desired end, of course, is to profit by mistakes and to repeat successes.

The more faith you put into the reading of this book, the more help you will get out of it, so let us consider, before going into the body of the book, a few facts that you already know, and do believe in surely. The reason for this approach will be seen and, I believe, appreciated later.

Most of us are familiar with case histories of people changing drab, frustrated lives into lives of brilliant usefulness, from poverty to financial success, from sickness to health, changing from loneliness to love and friendships, from criminal and anti-social attitudes into social conscience and law-abiding attitudes, with the aid of psychology and psychiatry. We know that most physi-

cians use psychology quite as much as medicine to effect
a cure in their patients. In fact, there is a branch of medicine called psychosomatic medicine. Yet we too often
forget that every sound principle in these miracle-working
sciences is also in the Bible, and that all such mental healings depend upon the same three principles involved in
scientific prayer—principles which anyone can learn and
use and which we shall discuss in this book.

Again, we know that throughout the ages the great
men and women who have made constructive history, who
have formed good governments or held them together in
times of great danger, who have eased the burdens of
mankind and given a new light and new hope to the world,
have always been men and women who had a religion
they believed in, and who knew how to pray.

Certainly we know that the great poets have always
sung of God and man's relation to Him, and of the possibility and desirability of man touching God through
prayer. Tennyson says,

"Speak to Him, thou, for He hears, and Spirit with Spirit
    can meet—
  Closer is He than breathing, and nearer than hands and
    feet."

Robert Browning agrees with Jesus that the Kingdom
of God is in man, that it is a mistake to try to find it from
without, and that the problem lies rather in our "opening
out a way whence the imprisoned splendor may escape."

Our daily papers and magazines are constantly carrying stories of the miracles of prayer. We have too many
authenticated accounts of men in the armed forces who
have found themselves while in a muddy shell hole, in the
green steamy jungle, adrift in mid-Pacific, or cast up on
a lonely island, lost, but for the power of prayer, ever
again to doubt that prayer is a power which man can use

at any time he cares to do so. Every minister, if he would, could tell of the miracles wrought by prayer. There would hardly be a church in existence were it not for the power of prayer.

If prayer can be used by some individuals to save and enrich their lives, why not by all? Why not by whole nations of people, to the end that we remake our world more to our ideals? Emerson said that all great ages were ages of belief. Why can't every man make every age of his individual life an "age of belief?"

Why do we see so much misery all around us, if this possibility of prayer is open to all? Why don't we use it in our economic life to achieve a more abundant life for all? Why don't we use it to create harmony and love between nations and men; to end war and strife; to reach out above our petty everyday affairs to a greater, grander wisdom?

Why? I am convinced the reason is that prayer is the least understood of all the powers known to man, and this, by reason of the fact that we are mentally lazy. We do not try hard enough to learn the laws involved and how to use them—until we have suffered long enough to become grimly determined to do something about it. Or we are like the little school girl who prayed God to change the capital of Illinois from Springfield to Chicago, over night, because she had put it on her examination paper that way that day. We fail in a few attempts at prayer, or we ask foolishly and, receiving no answer, give up.

It will also help us, before going into the body of this book, to define some of the terms and clarify some of the ideas which form the whole background of effective prayer as I understand it, as I have worked with it, and as it is explained in case histories herein.

Contrary to long belief, God does not punish man,

ever. We live under spiritual laws which are self-operating. If we try to operate our lives, satisfy our desires, outside those laws, we hurt ourselves. It is like running against a barbed wire fence. The fence and the law hold.

Again, every thought we think, every word we speak produces in our lives, after its kind. Our every word brings back to us after its own nature, with or without our desire, unless we, in the meantime, say yet another word which counteracts the first one. Our words return to us, but we do not always recognize them as our own, for they have become conditions and affairs. For example, the psychosomatic doctor tells us that many accidents, cuts, falls, even automobile collisions and the like are "accidents with a purpose," which can be traced to emotion origins. Teachers of New Thought Religion tell us that *all* such accidents are directly traceable to thought patterns, which in turn have grown out of one's deepest attitude about life. The latter I accept as truth, arriving at that conclusion from my own experiments.

Words are live things. Even as Isaiah said, they always accomplish and never return unto us void.

Prayer is a *conscious effort to communicate with the Infinite Spirit of the Universe* which we commonly call God.

Prayer, as I see it, falls under three headings:

1. The prayer of petition or asking, the purpose of which is to have the Infinite Spirit move on our behalf. In this prayer we may ask for guidance, for things, or for conditions, which are here understood to include persons.

2. The prayer of thanksgiving or acknowledgment, the purpose of which is to relieve our feelings by pouring forth words or thoughts of worship to pay, in effect, our debt, or to acknowledge blessings received. It may, of course, cover gratitude for any of the things for which we pray, or for the mere joy of existence, or the awe-

inspiring experience of having been in touch with the Infinite.

3. The prayer of search, or the heart's honest desire simply to be assured that God does exist, a desire to draw near to and co-operate with the Infinite, without either asking or thanksgiving. This is the highest form of prayer and under it comes all honest effort or work toward an honest end. This prayer expresses the highest desire known to man, the desire for final wisdom, or Truth.

All these three are *conscious* prayers, and involve man's free will, or outer, or objective mind which is also called the mortal, or individual mind. The point to remember is that conscious prayer requires desire, decision, and action on the part of man.

Man is three. He is body, mind, and spirit, or body, mind, and soul. No man ever loses his inner, or soul contact with the great Infinite Spirit, God, for it not only created him but keeps him in existence. If we ever, for an instant, lost this contact with God, we would cease to be—not just to live, but cease to *be*. For how could any of us, by taking conscious thought about the matter, direct the chemicals in our blood how to carry on their work? Or how order the direction of digestion? Or how heal a wound, or mend a broken bone? Could we consciously direct conception, cell growth and division and instruct the developing foetus how to construct an eye or a hand or a brain cell? Herbert Spencer speaks of it thus, "The soul doth the body make."

The freeing and the enslaving truth is that we *do* have the power with our conscious, objective free-will mind to interfere, countermand the inner order, or soul; to say the word or commit the act which throws the whole orderly workings out of tune. This is our free-will likeness to God. In all the universe there is nothing so free as mortal man's free mind. Herein lie all our glory and all our shame, all our past mistakes, all our future hopes for a better way of life, a better world. It is a truth so tremendous that we cannot visualize the full future of man, once he has learned to use his power by making contact with his inner mind or soul, by using his outer free-will mind.

Our inner mind, or soul, is always in contact with God. This mind creates the human hand. But it is our individual free-will mind that determines whether we shall use that hand to slay or to assist our fellow men. When we learn to listen to these inner promptings of the soul, we create good. We cannot too often remember that all growth is from within. It is this inner mind that points out a better way of life than man has ever tried. We do not get our ideas for a better world by looking at the pitiful world we now inhabit. From within, the Son seeth what the Father doeth, as Jesus mentioned. All hope is from within. All inspirations, a spiraling up and ever up, are from within, which constantly tell man's outer mind what to do. But he has the divine right to disregard these promptings if he chooses. He always has the right to "deny Christ."

The reader will find references in the text to the "Christ Mind in you," and the "Christ Power" in you. Do not let this be confusing. Jesus of Nazareth was the greatest soul that has ever come to earth. His free-will or individual conscious mind was developed or advanced so far beyond anything that was before or has been since, that even now, nearly two thousand years later, we are only beginning to understand what He taught. He knew perfectly how to make contact with His inner mind or soul, and communicate with the Infinite Spirit. The people hearing Him and realizing that He was speaking Truth, called Him Teacher or Christ, which also means

Messiah. Hence, when we speak of using this inner power that is in all of us, and which Jesus referred to as the Kingdom of heaven, we naturally say Christ Mind or Christ Power.

Jesus called the Infinite Spirit, or God, the Father, and this power within Himself which He used at will He called the Son of the Father. But His mortal individual self He referred to as the "Son of man." This is also in keeping with many of the scientific explanations of today. To the reader interested in this particular field, I recommend Gustaf Stromberg's *The Soul of the Universe*.

But for our purposes here we need not go into those matters. It is enough to note that Jesus never once claimed a power for Himself that He did not also say belonged to all men. I have no doubt that the day is coming when every man born will be born with his outer conscious mind as far developed as was that of the man Jesus, the Christ. I have no doubt that every man so born will be able to communicate with the Infinite Spirit, just as Jesus promised. And I see no reason to doubt that man will, indeed, do even greater things than Jesus did, since ours is a growing universe.

We need not wait for that coming day, nor yet to understand all these scientific matters. We can use the very simple approach, come as little children, as Jesus advised, and learn that prayer is a power at man's disposal. For it is, and always has been, possible to communicate with God and to understand His will.

It is the hope of the writer that many readers will take the time and make the effort to try a prayer program as here suggested. And if only one such reader finds success and learns to change his life through prayer, then this book will have been justified.

Perhaps everyone finds that words are slow and clumsy vehicles by which to carry truths he longs to convey to others. I believe this is what Emerson meant when he spoke of our painful efforts to utter our secrets. Certainly the best part of this book can never be what I have said here, but what the words and experiences of others whose stories appear here cause the reader to think and know and feel. This will be done by the process of arousing in him what he already knows (within his own soul) and always has known, but what for a while his mortal mind has forgotten, in the heat and care of the days.

Prodigal son, if you are sick and weary of the conditions to which your way of life has brought you, forsake the husks, arise, by prayer, and go unto your Father. You will find Him waiting, and when you but start He will see you from afar off, and run to meet you. He will place on you a robe and a ring, symbols of wealth, and give you food, symbol of health and life, and make you welcome on your return. For it is not the Father who deserted you. It was your own free will, exercised through ignorance or fear, that led you away from your Father's house. Arise and return to Him. He waits.

May God bless the reading of these words to you.

STELLA TERRILL MANN

Los Angeles, California.

❖❖❖

CHAPTER ONE

The First Step in Prayer

THE EXPERIENCES which have come under my observation, as well as my own personal ones, lead me to believe there are three definite steps in successful prayer. Actually, there is no clear-cut separation between the three. But for clarity's sake and the better to understand prayer as a whole, we shall here speak of it as having three parts or steps.

Before you can use prayer to change your life, conditions, environment, or affairs, or achieve your heart's desire, whatever it may be, you must be able to answer these questions:

What do you want?

What do *you* want?

What do you *want?*

This is no idle repetition of words. Prayer is a science. We acknowledge electricity to be a force in nature which is bound by laws which must be known and within which we must operate before we can expect to get a desired result. We would not, for example, try to heat an electric iron the cord of which was badly broken, no matter how much power happened to be available in the power house. So in prayer that changes lives. We deal with law. In all of nature's laws, we must learn and obey them or they will not obey or serve us.

Our first step then, is in asking for *what* we want. If we do not understand this we fail. We then "ask amiss and receive not."

There are several ways in which we are quite likely to ask amiss. The most common way has to do with this first step—to be confused as to *what* our lack really is; to ask for a thing we neither want nor need—because it *appears* to be what we want. In so asking we miss the whole point, remain blind to the thing we really want and for which we should pray.

Here is an example: A young woman came to me for help in her writing efforts. She had been writing for two years and had not sold a line. She wanted prayer to help her sell her work.

"Every time I start a story," she said, "I pray earnestly that it will sell the first time out. When I mail it I pray again that it will be bought. Help me to pray, or treat, for the editors so they will willingly buy my work."

"We do not need to treat (pray for) the editors," I said. "We need to treat you. The editors are already willing to buy your material if you send them what they want. They want what their readers want. There never have been enough good stories, enough inspiring and helpful articles, enough good books for readers. If you can actually produce something readers want, the editors will certainly buy it."

"I can't agree with you," she said sadly. "It is just because there is so little space and it is filled by famous writers, leaving no chance for an unknown writer."

It was no use to tell her that she was wrong, that every famous writer was once a beginner. No use, at that stage, to point out to her that it would be impossible for her to succeed as long as she actually believed her statement. If she did not believe it, she was indulging in a dangerous practice—dividing her house. To say one thing while actually believing another is always a dangerous practice. But this young woman was in no state to be convinced.

Instead, I got her to reveal her reasons for wanting to write.

She was much surprised to discover she did not want to be a writer at all. She had no great message for the world, did not care to learn to paint word pictures, nor yet to report or analyze. What she really wanted was to earn money. She had heard that writing was an easy way. That much she confessed.

By probing deeper, however, we discovered that she did not want to earn money so much as she wanted to get away from an unhappy home life. She lived with her brother and his wife and ardently hated her sister-in-law, she said. Having no money of her own and never having been trained to earn her living, she felt she had to be supported by her brother and his wife.

The young woman soon saw she had been asking amiss when she prayed to be enabled to sell a story. We agreed to put aside the idea of her wanting to write in order to earn a living and be able to get away from an environment she did not like and into one she would like. We agreed to begin where we properly should—with what she *did* want and had a right to expect: her rightful place, work to do with adequate pay, peace, harmony, love, and happiness.

"Anything but housework," said the petitioner when we began trying to decide what her right work would be.

That was another stumbling block that had to be removed before we could proceed. I have found there can be no fuzzy thinking, no hidden hates and reservations when it comes to prayer. For in prayer you are asking, in effect, for God to use His wisdom and His ways to solve your problem. You have to believe that He can and will. We must not try to tell God what to do in order to answer our prayers. The girl in this case soon saw that there could not be a demonstration if she outlined and took matters into her own hands. We discovered she hated housework because she did it every day with the sister-in-law whom she hated.

Persistent questioning as to why she hated the housework and her sister-in-law brought up the truth—the girl actually hated herself. She was angry with herself because she had to accept her brother's support, and being honest at heart, she hated to do this because it robbed the brother's wife of things rightfully hers. Here again the girl had been indulging in a dangerous practice, that of living a lie.

The girl's real trouble was a sense of shame. She hated herself every day for not being self-supporting. She did not know that this self-hatred was the voice of the Infinite Spirit urging her to develop and use her own powers. She did not know that this self-hatred was a definite guide and warning, nor did she realize it was at the bottom of her physical feelings of ill health which she described as "getting nervous, tied in knots." She daily saved her face, bolstered her ego, by imagining she was making a sacrifice in accepting support from her brother. This also explained why her stories were not acceptable. They were all written around a mean woman who kept her husband's sister a slave.

It was a task to convince that girl she had something to give the world. In her own eyes she was a failure. She had, she wept, "Sunk so low that she was living off her younger brother and his wife," who was also younger than herself. Every soul comes to earth with all it needs with which to acquire all that it will need or desire. The girl was convinced of this fact only after I had proved to her what she had to offer. But I did prove it, and with her own words.

In working with people I always require their written life history which must include their early childhood training along religious and educational lines. It must also include emotional experiences such as hates, fears, unfulfilled desires, and ambitions. These histories invariably reveal their predominant thought pattern, which in turn is a clue to their real attitude toward life, regardless of what pretense they may be living at the time. Unconsciously their soul speaks through their written words, and the present trouble is revealed. The way to right the trouble is, of course, through prayer. And the history nearly always reveals talents or capacities to serve for which the world will gladly pay.

In the above case, the girl revealed a great love for children. Quite in keeping with the case, the girl discovered part of her self-hatred grew out of her feeling that if she were away and self-supporting, her brother and his wife would be enabled to have a family; that they did not have a child because they did not know how long she would be dependent upon them.

With all pretense and false ideas out of the way and with the desire clearly before us, we knew *what* to pray for and we set to work. The girl was soon employed in the home of a young attorney whose wife needed help with two young children. She was very happy there, discovering she liked home-making very much, which is a highly creative profession. Later she met and married an attorney friend of her employer's. Her only attempts at writing were in exchanging cooking recipes with her sister-in-law whom she not only learned to respect but to love. Respect and love, like charity, begin at home, within the heart of the individual. When the girl found self-respect and began looking through honest eyes at her real self, and dropped her game of pretense, she could the more clearly see the real worth of others.

If you are failing to demonstrate with respect to some particular problem, take it apart and keep asking yourself, "Why do I want it this particular way?" until you get at the bottom of it, to the bare final truth. Your trouble may be like that of the girl above. You may be asking amiss by failing to see exactly *what* you want.

Let us agree, then, that the first law in prayer is knowing exactly *what* you want.

As soon as you have come to a clear and honest decision as to *what* you want, you must next ask yourself whether your desire is spiritually legal. For the second way in which we often ask amiss when we pray, is in asking for definite things that are not in line with God's law of progressive good for all men.

That term is my own loose expression of the law that we all know is operating throughout the universe; the law which the great Infinite Spirit has established and by which It forever carries man forward on the road toward civilization and the final goal. Emerson speaks of this law as protecting men from each other's evil (ignorance) and points out that under it the purely selfish acts of men are turned into good for all. Such a law does exist. To ask contrary to this law is to ask amiss.

Let us consider this point more fully, for it is a most important one, and one of the largest stumbling blocks with which we have to deal in a prayer program. I personally have not seen a demonstration made (prayer answered) that resulted in harm to others while of benefit to one. I do not say that it cannot be done. For under certain circumstances it most certainly can be done. Prayer works according to law. Prayer can be a two-edged sword. Jesus demonstrated this fact when He withered the fig tree, for He used the same power to destroy that He used to heal. To take another example: We are aware of the fact that electricity can burn a house down quite as easily as it can heat bath water.

All men are brothers created by the one Father. Man

loses sight of this fact and often attempts to get benefits for himself that involve harm for others. The results of such attempts are only temporary at best and bring great trials and suffering in their wake, most of all to the one who brought them about. It is not the Father who punishes such a person; no, such a person punishes himself through his spiritually illegal dealing. Such a spiritual outlaw can harm those who have put themselves into his power either by unconscious racial thought acceptance, or by their individual wrong thinking.

All men know these things in their secret hearts, for man's soul is ever in contact with the Infinite Spirit which created it and of which it is a part. Every man knows what is good and what is evil. Even a child knows. We get this knowledge from our own souls. It is easy enough to obey the inner voice teachings when we are alone. It is easy enough to think of all men as brothers, and, in theory, to wish them well. But when we go into the world we fail to remember that if these men are brothers that they too know good from evil; they too have a "still small voice" of conscience. Through fear or ignorance, we mistrust their acts. More fear is aroused. Hate follows. We become entangled in conflicting emotions. Then trouble comes. We judge after appearances, and soon we are acting on what we think others will want us to do, or acting on what we fear others are going to do, forgetting our brotherhood. We no longer know what *we* want, what our souls direct. All is confusion and fear.

Here is an example of the above points:

An officer of the law came to me and said, "My complaint is of the law's delay. Even Hamlet complained of it. I'm talking about spiritual laws that have failed to work in time for me. All I ask is justice under the law."

His idea of justice was at fault. He feared he would lose his job unless certain facts became known to certain

people within a certain time and he felt justified in taking
any means to make those facts known in time—"Though
it might mean sending two men to prison," he admitted.

"And you don't even know they are guilty? What
about their innocent wives and children? It is not necessary for you to hurt others in order to make a living.
You must treat these men as brothers, for you are spiritual brothers. If your demands are less than good for all,
then in the long run you are harming and not helping
yourself. And as for spiritual law, it never is delayed.
It always acts on time."

"Justice ought to be done," he argued stubbornly.

"Justice shall be done," I agreed, "but not vengeance.
We shall demonstrate for a justice that includes justice
for all, even for those who you think have harmed you.
If we are to call spiritual law to our aid, we must come
with clean hands, just as we do in our man-made laws."

The officer finally admitted that he himself, in line with
the convictions of his own soul, did not want the two men
in question to go to prison. But there were other factions
in the complicated case and other men who did. Through
fear and resentment the officer had concluded that he
couldn't get the help he wanted (and felt justified in receiving) without "falling in line with the other faction,"
which would implicate the two men.

"Your desire for justice for others must equal your
desire for justice for yourself," I kept reminding him as
we worked. "Stop thinking about what the other people
in this muddle want and fear. Stay at home in your own
honest heart; consult your own soul. If you actually want
justice for all concerned, then you can call the law into
effect for yourself and nothing can keep it from working
for you."

The officer finally saw the truth that justice and mercy
are principles and not things and people, and that they

never vary or stretch to suit the situation or the petitioner. He finally saw that he need not even ask for justice because, like all spiritual laws, it is self-operating.
He had but to conduct himself so that he was in line with
the laws, and they would work in his affairs. We igno-
rantly or foolishly attempt to operate our lives and affairs contrary to the best interests of others, and so we
break not the law, but ourselves. God is One, the Father
of all, and never does He break a law, or favor one child
at the expense of another.

The officer finally got his case down to these words:
"God is not going to arrest (stop) me in anything I want
to do as long as I am within the law." Which was pure
truth. He came to see that there is no safety outside
spiritual laws, any more than there is outside man-made
laws. He was soon comparing the two laws, even to seeing that there can be liberty and justice only under law.

We set to work on the officer's problem, praying for
guidance and for a consciousness of the law. Soon he was
sent to another state to return an escaped prisoner. This,
he observed, "neatly lifted him out of the whole mess."
It was a solution which he "never would have dreamed of
in his own mind."

On his return, the officer said, "The law's delay was a
good thing at that," speaking of man-made laws. His
prisoner was innocent. But because he had once been in
prison, and because of other circumstances, he had not
been able to prove himself innocent. The officer gathered
facts to help his prisoner and got so interested in doing
so, he forgot his own problem, except that he kept knowing without a doubt (which is a high form of prayer)
that he did not have to worry; that his problem would
"turn out right for all concerned."

And it did. He got a new job which grew out of work
done for the prisoner. The condition which had so

aroused him came to a head, was discovered and cleared up, without costing him time, money, or unhappiness. Most important, he did not make a move that was against his own conscience. His demonstration came within the law of good. He had made his desire spiritually legal after he settled on what *he* wanted and not on what he thought others could or would force him to do. He said, "I never will ask the world's opinion again. I shall look in my own soul, consult God and not man."

Let us be agreed then, that we never are to ask for a private benefit which will work a public harm. If it is a good thing, it will bless all in ever widening circles. If it will not bless all, then we are somehow asking amiss and we must look into the matter carefully, remembering all men are brothers.

A third way in which we often ask amiss when we pray, is to fail to be sure of what we *want*. This means what we really lack or actually have need of.

It is easy to ask for more than we are using, to look toward a future desire, failing to see or use what is already at hand. This is proof of failure to be thankful. We must use what we have in order to get more. We must be thankful and be willing to take the first step in solving our present problem.

This example comes to mind:

A woman came to me for help in demonstrating money. She wanted her aunt, a wealthy widow, to give her three thousand dollars with which to buy a little home. Fearing the aunt might marry the attorney who was handling her affairs and have her fortune squandered, she also wanted their relationship broken up.

The woman had not asked her aunt for a gift or a loan. "She is so mean and stingy and so bad-tempered I can't ask her! She never would do it anyhow."

"You don't need my help," I said. "Your prayer, the

thing you most ardently believe in, is being answered. You do not expect her to help you and she has not done so. Let's forget the aunt and work on you. In order to receive you must first give. It is the law. Now, what do you have to give your aunt, or the world, that no one else can give so well?"

"Nothing! We are poor. We have four young children. Auntie lives in a big house with servants and has more money than she knows what to do with! That crooked attorney is making her believe he loves her. She goes out with him because she is lonely. She . . ."

"How much money would she have to spend to buy genuine appreciation, genuine love, genuine companionship and admiration from her only living relatives?" I interrupted. "She has a right to expect such love from you without paying for it with money."

The woman blushed, understanding me perfectly. She was surprised to find how much she had to offer the aunt. "Practice Truth living on her," I said. "Do not look to her for money or help of any kind. Look to the great Infinite Spirit around you which created heaven and earth and is never bankrupt either of goods or ideas. Give to your aunt; give love, appreciation. Go out of your way to find her good qualities, for being a child of God she does have them."

"I don't see why I have to be so nice to her when she . . ."

"Because she is apparently the only person that you do not like. You do not really dislike the aunt. You are cross and angry with yourself because you have not acquired a home and other luxuries and necessities to which you know you are entitled. You have not used all the talents and capacities God has given you. But since it is nearly impossible for us to admit our own short-comings and to place the blame where it belongs, we are proficient in saving face and in blaming another, whom we can then hate conveniently."

"You mean then, that as long as I hate and blame auntie, I will not make the effort to right my own life?"

"Exactly. She serves as a scapegoat. Learn to truly love and appreciate her and you will no longer hate yourself. Moreover, you will find the way to get the home you want and have a right to expect. Awaken your own soul. Learn to speak through it to everyone you meet. Give thanks for all that you already have. This will open your eyes to new opportunities."

The woman discovered how much she already had of love, comfort and happiness. She had a good husband and four wonderful children. She learned to give thanks for her hands while working, for her eyes when she read, for every cent that passed through her fingers, for a thousand blessings of which she had not before been conscious.

The woman made a sincere effort even after her husband one day remarked, "You used to run your aunt down all the time, now you have nothing but praise for her. What's got into you?" Still the aunt did not give them money. But they got a home. The four children became very fond of the aunt whose disposition improved like magic, according to her niece. More money flowed into the home, but not a cent came from the aunt. The woman and her family continued their program of prayer and thanksgiving until they outgrew any need of the aunt. Then they began to discover how much they really liked her, and how much they could do for her and took joy in doing. Later, the aunt went to live with this niece and her family, saying they were the only people in the world who really loved her for herself alone, the only ones who made her think life was worth while. This arrangement grew into a situation good for all concerned, beyond the dream of any of them; a situation that never could have come into existence had the woman got the three thousand dollars when she wanted it.

This woman did not need money, but a knowledge of spiritual laws and how they work. She had to learn to love in order to be loved; to give in order to receive. She did not need the aunt's love, but she did need to give the aunt her love. She did not need to change the aunt; she did need to change her own ideas of life, including her ideas about the aunt. Basically, her problem was not how to get but how to give. Her prayer was not, "Give me, oh Lord," but "Teach me to be grateful, make me more and more aware of the great good I have to give."

There is no problem which necessitates our changing the other person. That is up to him and his own soul. We do not need to reform the world. We need to reform ourselves. Once we learn to count our blessings they increase. Gratitude keeps good in circulation. When we learn to change ourselves, the problem of having to change another vanishes.

Before going on to the next chapter where we shall discuss the second step in our prayer program, which is faith, let us review what we have just learned.

The first step in effective prayer is to ask aright and not amiss. We ask amiss when our purposes are confused, or when we are afraid or ashamed to face the real issue and come to an honest admission of *what* we really want. We can test this by checking up on whether our answer depends upon certain people, places or things. It should depend on principles.

We ask amiss if we ask outside the law of progressive good for all mankind. We must be spiritually lawful in our desires and not ask for a private good that will do a public harm, or that we hope will carry us forward, or give us advantages over others by holding them back. For every soul has the right to freedom and to growth and God does not play favorites. There are none chosen above the others, neither individuals nor races.

We must be honest with our own inner consciences and ask what *we* want and not what we think we are forced to want simply because we see no other way out of the difficulty, or because we are afraid to act in line with our own consciences.

We ask amiss if we fail to count our blessings in order to keep them alive and in circulation. We ask amiss if we refuse to take the first step, to give first, and to forgive. Before praying we should earnestly ask ourselves, "Do I truly lack what I ask, or is it another lack which I myself can supply but am unwilling to do so?"

We are now ready to discuss faith, the second step in prayer.

CHAPTER TWO

The Second Step in Prayer

FOR THE SAKE of clarity, we have said there are three steps in making a demonstration or bringing into reality the desires of our hearts by the means of prayer. The first, we said, is in asking aright and not amiss.

The second step in our program of prayer is believing, or faith. "Ask what ye will, and it shall be done unto you," was Jesus' promise. Also, "Whatsoever you shall ask in prayer, believing, you shall receive." Further, "All things are possible to him that believeth." Thus spoke Jesus, who knew more about prayer than anyone else who ever lived.

Properly considered, believing is really the sum and substance of all prayer. In referring to it here as the second step in demonstration we mean rather a quickening of our dormant faith into active faith that our present problems can and will be solved.

People have more faith than they actively use. The fact that we pray at all indicates our underlying faith in God or a Supreme Being, in someone or something that hears and answers prayers. This must be a permanent part of our consciousness or we not only would not attempt to pray, but would scarcely attempt any of the complicated processes of life on earth. Without faith that the seeds will grow and produce after their kind, the farmer would grow no crops. If we had enough faith all the time and used it all the time, we should not have to be concerned about how to demonstrate at particular times, for life would be a constant demonstration of orderly good, constantly progressing in growth of the soul toward its ultimate.

Jesus' faith was constant. Yet when it came to specific problems, Jesus reiterated His faith. He always gave thanks, and He made His requests in definite, precise words. We can do the same when we learn how. When Jesus raised Lazarus from the dead He first gave thanks that He had been heard. This showed faith of the highest order. He said, "I knew that thou hearest me always," showing that He was not trying to whip up faith for the instant, but that He had long had it. "I knew," shows us His faith was both constant and immediate.

It seems that Jesus Himself could not heal or help when the petitioner had no faith. You remember the "man in authority" who came to have his servant healed had so much faith that he told Jesus it wasn't necessary for the Master to go to the servant, but to "only say the word." This man was himself an authority in his sphere, used to ordering men to go and come, and used to being obeyed. He instantly realized that Jesus was working on a plane which he did not understand, but he knew without doubt that Jesus well knew what He was doing. Jesus commented on the man's faith, and we read that this man's servant was healed in that same hour. Again, it was not Jesus' robe that healed the woman when she touched the hem of it, but her faith, said Jesus. How many other sick people do you suppose were in that same jostling crowd that day, who did not have faith and so were not healed. Many must have touched Him, must have come close enough to have asked His blessing. Yet they were not healed, or at least we have no record of it. The woman went out with a set purpose, a definite plan, an overpowering faith that if she could but "touch the hem" of His garment, she would be healed. No need to speak, to beg, to explain. Faith made her whole.

Believing is not begging or demanding or crying for or worrying about. Believing is not putting forth will power. Believing is a knowing beyond any doubt whatever that God exists and that He is our Creator, the great Infinite Spirit that guides and protects us. It is remarkable that in some degree all human beings have this faith. Their god may be a totem pole, a graven image or the living God, but all believe in something outside themselves as having power greater than their own, capable of helping them in time of trouble.

How can we quicken this dormant faith? How can we step it up, so that in times of trouble, it acts on our behalf? By thinking about it. By speaking affirmations and by using our outer conscious mind for the purpose of cooperating with our inner Christ mind.

We must never forget that Jesus never once claimed a power for Himself that He did not also claim for you and me—all men. Plainly He said that we, you and I, could do anything that He did if we learned the "will of the Father," which meant the way the laws work. There is nothing mysterious in the power Jesus used. Theology has built up mystery and confusion about the so-called miracles of Jesus, which were not supernatural at all but quite the opposite. They were workings of the law, just as using electricity to light a room is a working of natural laws.

In trying to quicken our faith for the task at hand, it will help us to consider faith as a whole. The faith that moves mountains is a steady, unwavering certitude that ours is a universe of law, love, and plenty. Such a conviction gives power and peace and directs acts toward success in any undertaking.

What we need to learn is how to open our whole beings

to the inflow of universal ideas of good, riches and health. We must invite such thoughts, and induce our thoughts to dwell on such ideas. For faith is a becoming aware of God and of our own immortality. This relation between God and man is one that always has existed, and man always has known of this relationship. But since the "fall of man," since the forgetting, man has strayed far afield in his ideas regarding this relationship. The higher and brighter the inner flame of awareness burns, the more sure is our demonstration. We do not have to beg God, we have but to *know* God.

Our little problems close in on us so tightly that it often is difficult for us to see out and over them to the reality, the entire picture. Yet we have but to look around us to see that ours is a universe of law, love, beauty, perfection, and a constant supply of all that is necessary to maintain and further life on earth. We have but to consider the laws of mathematics, chemistry, physics, and to consider facts of astronomy, to be convinced that all is cosmos and not chaos. This should lead us to believe that the forces which govern our lives are no hit-and-miss affairs but absolute laws, and that we can learn these the same as we learn the laws of gravitation, for example.

For an enlarging of faith, and an increase of self-respect, I recommend such books as *The Expanding Universe,* by Arthur Stanley Eddington, *The Universe Around Us,* by Sir James Jeans, and *Man the Unknown,* by Dr. Alexis Carrel. Almost any of the many good books on psychology and psychiatry will help to convince the reader that the Bible's statement that "as a man thinketh, so is he," is pure truth. Faith does not have to come in a lump sum. It can be built by anyone who cares to take the time to do so.

I agree with Franklin that we need a religion which admits of questions. One of the reasons modern science has discovered so much and harnessed so much power for man's use, from electricity to plastics, is that scientific men dare to question former authority. We know a great deal of the story of man on earth. We know, through science, some of the *when* and *where,* much of the *how,* but of the *why* we know little as yet. But we need not. It is enough for us to become as little children in this approach, just as Jesus advised us to do, and to think of this great force, or Supreme Power, as a Father.

We can build up mountain-moving faith if we think of the Supreme Power as a kind, loving, all-wise Father who knows, indeed, what things we have need of, even before we ask. In fact, recorded history shows us that our needs are met long before we know the need will exist. Every new good that has come to mankind has had to be slowly, painfully sold to him. He has, almost without exception, refused every new good that came. Consider the struggle of Morse to convince mankind that the telegraph was a new good for the world. Harvey was not believed when he said the blood circulated. Pasteur was not believed when he showed a new way to save lives. We did not even believe in the "horseless carriage," nor could we look ahead to the day when it would be a grim necessity and not a freak oddity.

Always, mankind's needs have been met. God works through men who have faith, patience, determination. By their work, their faith, they communicate with God, ask their questions of nature, or the problem at hand, and through their ideas, which are God's messengers, they receive their answers. Every honest, purposeful question of the nature of things, is an attempt to communicate with God.

God's laws, the laws of nature, are just, beyond our human power fully to understand. Except for love, why should this Infinite Spirit we call God have created us, given us intelligence, a part to play in His plans, and implanted in us the urge to live, to love, and to grow, so that we would want to co-operate with that plan? When we can come to see that man cannot fail if he will but ask and listen, we shall be well on our way to the faith that Jesus had. And we shall be just as able to use it.

A working faith must take in all of life and conditions. Man has ever feared the end of things, being cut off from life by being cut off from the things which maintain physical life. Man has always been afraid of starving to death. There has long, perhaps always, been a universal belief in limitation—that there is not enough of things to go around. Yet in no place is nature limited. We see this in the sands of the sea, in the sunlight, in the seed pods, in the recreating processes of nature going on about us all the time. Rich mother nature! More prolific, more productive, extravagant, wasteful, than man ever dared to be. All man's riches come from understanding this prolific abundance of nature and from working wisely with it. In simpler words, to be conscious of God is to have faith that enables one to accept the riches of life.

Jesus tried to convince His followers (who include you and me) that all that the Father has belongs to us for the asking and taking. He said it was done unto us as we believed. He didn't say we had to go out and struggle and fight, steal from each other, murder, pass laws of limitation in order to get what we need to live and grow. The whole difference between great abundance in life and tragic poverty is a difference of belief.

Back of poverty is a belief in poverty or a law of limitation that is opposed to the true condition of the law of plenty. It is not the laws of nature, God, which bind man to poverty, but the laws of man's own thinking. Every thought creates after its kind. Who doubts that China or India could be as richly productive as America, were the peoples of those countries to think the American way? Americans think the way they do because our form of government is based on Christian Principles, on the worth and rights of the individual. Americans were born into race thoughts of freedom of the individual, of individual effort being the way to success and riches, and of brotherly love being good business ethics. When we talk about changing our lives through prayer, we must consider man's thoughts as a whole, his attitude, and not just a few selected thoughts now and then. For we shall come to see that all earnest thought is prayer.

Take it as absolute truth that every thought creates after its kind. The only law of supply is the law of abundance, just as the only law of light and energy is the incessant radiation of the sun. Darkness is absence of light, but is nothing in itself, has no weight, no power, can neither think nor act. Poverty likewise is nothing in itself. Yet more prayers are offered up that have grown out of a belief in the reality of poverty than in almost anything else. We just cannot, it seems, develop a working faith that will insure a constant supply. But here and there is a man or woman whose faith is so large that it brings in abundance for him or her, and for thousands of others in an ever widening circle.

Faith is a belief that all good things are ours now if we will but recognize the fact and act accordingly. When our faith burns brightly we seem to have few problems. We meet with experiences, but they are not "problems." They are but new opportunities to grow. But when our faith grows dim, when we forget for long spaces of time to draw near to God, to pray daily, to be thankful daily, then problems arise. These problems are also experiences, new opportunities to grow. But because we have left the path of peace and have taken the path of fear and worry—have let go of God's hand—we are suddenly alone, afraid, and poverty-stricken.

There are three ways in which most of us break up and scatter our power of faith in normal times and fail to generate it at critical times, at times when we are attempting to demonstrate. Let us now consider the first one.

First, we listen to old race fears instead of listening to our own still small voice of faith and common sense. It is good to say "Lord, I believe; help Thou mine unbelief." If no other thought than our own reached us or influenced us, or if only the high-faith thoughts of others reached us, building up mountain-moving faith would be easier.

But the race thoughts are there. They come to us in old adages, folk tales, accepted customs, beliefs, and superstitions. They come back to us through our childhood fears, our parents' fears, old memories of seeing others fail and suffer. Every event of our lives, every line we have read, every word we have listened to, has its effect on our lives in accordance with what we have accepted or rejected concerning it.

Second, we listen to the current race fears around us. We listen to the neighbors, the family, the boss, the newspapers, to the radio gossip, and we adopt the fears there voiced. For days and weeks on end, if we are not careful, we forget God or the power of all good; like the prodigal son, we go wandering far afield away from our Father's house into a strange country. And like him we are soon eating husks.

A third way in which we cut off our faith, or let ourselves be separated from God and reality, is by looking at appearances and judging after them. We make the mistake of accepting appearances as final, real, unchangeable and fixed forever. Jesus warned us not to judge by appearances. He did not deny appearances. He just paid no attention to them and busied Himself in calling on God, or the law, for what He wanted, regardless of the appearances. He did not accept appearances as the final state of affairs.

We let the very room we are in convince us of poverty; the very furniture convince us of ugliness in a world that should be beautiful. The bills on the desk, the medicine in the cabinet, the threats of the future, all affect and tear down our faith by their very appearances. We should see past them to what we *do* want.

When people come to me for help, I insist we settle this question of the second step, of believing or faith, as soon as we have settled the first one of knowing what to ask for. The following case covers the three mistakes we have been discussing and it also shows the importance of keeping faith at a high pitch all the time, instead of waiting until something happens.

A woman came for help in demonstrating a job for her husband. She had been praying alone; she had frequently had prayers answered, but this time, she said, she was "absolutely stuck," and going on Jesus' promise that where two should agree on a thing it should be done unto them, she had come to me to work with her.

After going into the woman's problem I had her draw an outline of a pair of scales and label it "The Scales of Justice." This was to remind us as we worked that God's laws are just; that it is done unto us as we believe. On one side of the scales I had her write, "I want," and on the other, "I do not want." These sides of the scales represented the reality and the appearances, respectively, of her problem. Then we reviewed the means she had used during a typical day of working with her problem.

At nine in the morning, when her children had been sent off to school and her husband was out job hunting, the woman began her prayer by reading and meditation. By ten she would be imbued with the belief that her prayer could be and would be answered. She would believe there was plenty for all—that God, her Creator, would supply her family's need and that this would be done, whether she knew how it would be done or not. I had her write "one hour" on the "I want" side of the scales. For this one hour she had not been accepting appearances; her faith had been high enough to carry her past appearances to what she wanted.

At ten the woman had been in the habit of stopping her prayers and turning on the radio while doing her housework. War news, and dramatic plays featuring unhappiness, bad luck, and tragedy, would fill her ears and thus her thoughts, until twelve. By that time she would be physically tired and mentally receptive to her husband's discouragement when he came in for lunch. I required her to put "three hours" on the side of the scales representing appearances, or things she did not want.

By one, after the three hours on the wrong side of thought were up, the husband would again be out job hunting, the woman at her work. She would not recover easily from the discouragement of the lunch hour. Neither of them had high faith, so each of them unconsciously robbed the other of the little faith he did have. After lunch, a long-faced and long-winded neighbor would appear to visit and sympathize with the woman who was "having such a hard time, poor dear." She was bursting, moreover, with fears of many sorts which she reported dolefully.

At three the children would come home from school, before the woman had yet recovered from her session with the neighbor's fears. As the children ate and laughed and talked happily about things they needed in their particular world of interests, the mother could not see them receiving these things. Her faith was so low by that time that she would worry lest there might not be any lunch for them a week hence. She was accepting appearances.

While preparing dinner and later while washing dishes, the woman would worry some more. She would not stop worrying until nine at night, when the family was in bed. Then she would sit down alone to read and pray and meditate. She would retire at ten, again sure her prayer for supply of needed things would be answered.

When we tallied up all the waking hours, we found that the woman had spent only two hours in praying for what she really wanted, and in her thoughts, fears, worries and negative beliefs—at least eleven hours—in praying for what she most certainly did not want. But what she most surely believed in! To believe in a thing is to order it, or command it to appear in our lives. We do not get what we pray for, but what we *believe* we shall receive.

With the record before her on paper, the woman saw that the law was just, that she herself had tipped the scales on the side of defeat. She saw then that we must pray without ceasing, work without stopping, and think without pausing, for good, for ideas grounded in faith that God exists, that man cannot fail.

When we learn to live by faith and not by fear, even fifty-one per cent of the time, we shall make over our lives and affairs. Until we do so learn we are likely to lead a drab existence, which is all hope one day, all fear the next.

I have found it helpful, in working with those who find faith wavering, to go repeatedly into the reasons behind their desire, the thing for which they pray, and get at the real reason behind their fear that it will not be granted. Sometimes it is a feeling that an answer to their prayer would rob or cheat another. They have to learn there is plenty for all and to spare, here and now. The great Infinite Spirit which created the world surely is not bankrupt. Jesus never preached scarcity. He proved that He needed only His word, spoken in faith, to multiply what there was in sight, to all that He needed to meet a present problem. What we see is the merest fraction of what there is. That we can multiply our good by our own words is the real lesson in the loaves and fishes demonstration.

Sometimes the petitioner feels he does not deserve what he asks for, even when it is a good and right thing. That feeling has to be replaced with the knowledge that we are the only channels through which God is able to carry on His work on earth, as beings made in His own image and likeness. I have never seen a right demonstration fail when the petitioner was convinced that God had need of him and his work. This is faith of a high order, faith that we belong to God and to the scheme of things.

Many petitioners have failed in their prayer programs because they could not believe they were important to God or to the scheme of things. I have discovered cases where the trouble began in early childhood when the petitioner suffered an experience which made him feel unwanted and shoved aside; or a sense of being inadequate, less than others around him, or in some way very markedly different which meant less. One case was that of a woman who never had married. As a very young child she had once worn a red flannel petticoat to school. It had become wet and it stained through her outer skirt. The children teased. The boys snickered. She was "embarrassed to the soul," she confessed. She hugged that sense of shame and disgrace tightly to her the rest of her life. It went from stained skirt to ideas of something wrong with her life, compared with others, and on to a thinking that there was no God, and if one, certainly not for her. Unfriendly acts of the little school children grew in her mind to fixed ideas of an unfriendly Universe.

Faith is an all-over process. It must touch every phase of our life. If our faith is shallow, we are tripped and thrown out of step by every new phase of life with which we are confronted. If our faith is deep and constant, we see every such change as a chance for growth and we thank God for it. For the purpose of all life is growth. Only new situations permit growth. We must learn to be happy when they present themselves, and to welcome them for the blessings they are.

For example: A few years ago a young woman pianist came to me, asking me to sign a petition to keep the "canned music" out of all motion-picture theaters. For years she had earned her living by playing the piano for silent pictures. Then came the "talkies" and with them the "canned music." The new method, she wailed, would throw thousands of organists, pianists, and other musicians out of work. She was as much interested in the fate of her fellow musicians as she was in her own problem. She wanted all petition signers to refuse to go to a motion picture theater that did not employ live musicians.

In refusing to sign the petition, I said, "I do not believe in trying to limit God. This new idea is a God idea and as such will bless all. In God we grow. We are held back only by our own stubborn fears. Neither you nor I nor a whole organization can hold back one God idea that is needed on earth, any more than the fearful could stop Galileo from making his discoveries. Your desire to have me sign the petition is founded on your mistaken and foolish fear that God is poor; that He can no longer feed you and your fellow musicians." She was soon laughing at her own fears.

That was a clear example of trying to hold back progress and good for all, for the benefit of a few. It was an example too of dormant weak faith in God, or the law of progressive good and growth for all. It was a belief in poverty and limitation as opposed to a belief in plenty. These two ideas have always been at war in the world. We see them in our social, economic, and political life to-day. We see them as motivating ideas of different races and nations. Two ideas: only one of them can be true. The truth is that the purpose of *all* life is growth. The people who draw near to God and ask and receive ideas are the ones who win, always, whether they are asking for the secrets of the atom or the best way to grow apples. The fact we most often forget is that we do not have to fight with, or overcome, the people holding the opposite idea. No, we have but to strengthen our own faith; we have to fight our own fears. We have to get right with the law.

There is no way to stop the law of plenty and progress from working. It is God's law, carrying us forward. If we have faith that all is good we put ourselves into the full flood of it and are carried along with it. We receive ideas, see ways and means to solve problems, see ways to create great good for all. If we lack such faith, we balk and try to hold back and hurt ourselves. What hurts, teaches. Eventually we learn.

In trying to build up faith do not assume the worm-of-the-dust humility. No child of the great Infinite Spirit has a right to pretend to be so little. Think well of yourself. You can afford to. You are here on earth to do a certain work. God had need of you or you wouldn't be here. You have been given the tools, the abilities, with which to do your work. You were also given the desire to do certain things. It may be covered over with fear or neglect, but it is there. It is safe to say that God wants you to succeed far more than you could possibly want to. Did you give yourself your desire? No, certainly not.

Where did it come from? God, of course. Then why worry? Have faith, and get to work.

When we have developed enough faith in God and in the divine meaning of the universe, we shall not pray, asking, but simply recognize our place and act accordingly.

As it is, our faith works more by fits and starts. The comforting thing is that the power of faith is a cumulative power. Every time we see clearly that God is the source of all, that all is good, and that only our own thinking about things makes them evil or bad, we have built up the total weight of our faith. We can the better see how we build faith if we compare our faith structure to a brick building. Each experience is a brick. Our faith is the mortar that holds the brick in place.

When we have enough faith, it automatically carries us through the third step in our prayer program which we shall discuss in the next chapter as "waiting on the Lord." We must remember, of course, that these three steps are really part of a unified action and are considered apart from each other only for the purpose of study.

Before we go into that third step, let us briefly review what we have already learned: Prayer is a *conscious desire* or *attempt to communicate* with the *Infinite Spirit* which created the Universe—the only Power which we also call God. Since all the Universe is law and order, we realize that prayer, the method of communication, must also belong to law and order. Anyone who can think can pray. He who learns to think correctly, uses the law to his benefit.

If we are to change our lives from what they are to what we want them to be, or move God to act in our behalf, we must learn to pray aright and not amiss. This consists in knowing *what* we want, what *we* want and what we *want,* or actually lack. Then, we must ask in faith, believing. This means not only a faith that Divine Mind will hear and answer our prayer, but also a total faith in the universe around us; a faith that we are a part of the scheme of things, needed and wanted, and so, guided and protected to the end that we will co-operate with God's great plan for man.

Finally, by our very desire to lead better lives, to treat our fellow men well, to do no harm to anyone, to give the freedom to others that we want for ourselves, we show faith in God and our willingness to co-operate with His plan.

People are more religious than they know, and all of us have more faith than we are using. Unconsciously, we all believe in the power of prayer. It is our conscious or outer mind that creates doubts. We grow too dependent on our physical senses for evidence of things. No one has ever seen a thought, or touched or tasted or smelled or heard one. But we see every day of our lives where thought has been at work, and we see the kind of thought it was by the work it has done. We have but to look at the lines in the face of the drunkard stumbling out of a night club to know his life history. If we compare such a face with that of Lincoln, we can see that it is the intangibles, the unseen forces, which really do the work in this world, and not the outside things, visible to physical eyes.

We shall come to see that every thought is a belief, a prayer.

We are now ready to discuss the third step in prayer, that of "waiting on the Lord."

CHAPTER THREE

The Third Step in Prayer

THE FIRST TWO STEPS in prayer are asking aright and asking in faith, believing. The third step is what I term "waiting on the Lord."

One does not consciously have to go through the whole mental process. No, but every life-changing prayer is made up of those three parts, whether recognized or not, just as walking is made up of desire, decision, and motivation. We seldom stop to think it out that way, but once we did. We had to in order to learn.

Living by prayer can become as automatic as walking or eating. We can afford to forget the parts when we've learned them thoroughly and have done them so often there is no hitch between them; when we go from desire to decision to action as a whole, instead of considering each separate part.

Let us now look at this third step of prayer. What does it mean to "wait on the Lord?"

To wait, says Webster, means to "look (mentally); to be in expectation; to be or remain ready to serve or execute orders; to act as attendant or servant." That definition contains the three essentials of the third step of prayer. Most of us fail in one or more of them.

First, we forget to allow for the element of time, and growing fearful or anxious, we dig up our planted seed. Next we fail to "be in expectation" of God's answer. We doubt. We hurry and worry and end up trying to do it ourselves in our own way. Lastly, we forget to "be or remain ready to execute orders; to act as attendant or servant."

Each of these essentials deserves separate consideration. Take the element of time in waiting on the Lord. We observe this element of time as present in everything in the universe. Some things seem to happen as swiftly as light. Again, we realize and make allowance for the fact that it takes time to produce an apple from an apple blossom, to build a house from felled trees. It even takes time to turn the most naturally talented singer into an opera star.

Our confusion grows out of the fact that it takes but an instant to get an idea, to wish or want or ask for something. So when it comes to looking for answers to our problems, we are impatient of time. We do not dig up a radish seed to see if the laws of nature are being kept, but we forget to "wait on the Lord" when we plant a spiritual seed.

We fail "to be in expectation" of God's answer when we grow impatient and try to do the job ourselves in our own way. If we want an electric iron to heat up we first make sure all the apparatus involved is in working order. We plug in. The iron begins to heat. If we tested it too soon and decided the electricity could not heat, we would be ignoring the element of time. To get impatient, pull the plug, break the connection and decide to heat the iron over a gas flame instead, would be failing to expect the law to work.

But it is our failing to wait on the Lord or to be a servant unto Him that is so often overlooked. If we are absolutely honest about it, we shall have to admit there are many times when we fail "to be or remain ready to serve" or to "act as attendant or servant."

If we are servants of the Lord, we know there is small use to come asking good for ourselves while we entertain hatred in our heart or a desire for revenge or punishment against another. Jesus warned and instructed, "Forgive us our debts as we forgive our debtors." It is the law, and if we are to use it in our behalf, we must comply with its tenets.

There is yet another factor which we must consider here. When Jesus gave us the Lord's prayer, He was showing us how to understand the laws involved, and how to use them. "Thy kingdom come, Thy will be done on earth as it is in heaven," is a statement of the law and how to use it. Jesus said that the kingdom of God was within us. He called Himself and all of us Sons of God. This means that there is a power within us which is never separated from God, for it is a part of God. Our trouble comes in not knowing how to use it.

It is this very God Mind within us, which teaches us from within. It is this power which is at work when we feel the need of a better life, a better way of life for all men than any man has yet tried. It is from this same power that we receive ideas on how to make life better, after the desire to do so has been aroused. Hence, when we say "Thy will be done on earth as it is in heaven," we are saying we are willing to do our part to make manifest on earth these inner dreams and desires of our own higher self. We are also saying that we quite realize that our own individual mortal minds cannot cope with the problem at hand. We are saying that we are willing and anxious for God to work through us. Which implies, or should imply, our willingness to "wait on the Lord."

The following case covers all three main divisions of prayer, asking aright, asking in faith, and waiting on the Lord.

A man and his wife came to me for help in getting a loan to buy a small grocery store. The man had lost his own, having been forced out of business by a big chain store that came to his neighborhood.

We began with the first step, deciding by the method of analysis just what to ask for. "Even if I got another store," the man said unhappily during the questioning, "I would just go broke again. There is no longer any place left for the small business man; no longer any need of him."

He had voiced a deep bitterness that had to be eliminated before we could go further. We talked about the law that forever keeps man moving forward. After a while he was able to say, "The chain stores have proved a blessing to many and are good for everybody but the individual small-store owner, perhaps."

"But progress does not of necessity hurt anyone," I declared. "It means growth for all and is a law of nature. If you have been shoved out of one job, then you are ready for another. It is not what has happened that is hurting you, but only what you are thinking about it. It is not a loan you want, for that would be asking amiss. What you want and have a right to expect is your rightful place, your constant and abundant supply of all good. For these will permit your soul growth. The purpose of all life is growth. But to demonstrate the right circumstances you must believe that there is another place, that supply is rightly yours, that leaving one type of work does not mean there is no other, but rather another and better."

The man had been a farmer. Questioning revealed the fact that he was not so much interested in operating a grocery store as he was in food itself. He loved to think about food, talk about it, from seed to soil, through growing and packing to putting it on the table, and he had an unusual fund of knowledge about foods in general.

Personally, I can help people only when I can apply

the teachings of Jesus' spiritual laws to things they already know and believe in as law. From there we work on to the next step. With this man I began our talk about asking in faith by discussing the laws of nature that he knew and already believed in. For at that time he did not know much about spiritual laws; that is, he had not identified spiritual and natural law as two parts of a whole.

This man could not believe that there "is anything that hears prayers and desires and does something about it." I said, "You do believe there is a power that operates in such a way that the seed takes what it needs from the soil, the sun, the air, and the water in order to develop to its desired end, don't you?"

"Of course," he admitted, surprised that anyone should question it. "Moreover," he added, "I am sure the seed has intelligence enough for its need just as a cow or chicken has intelligence enough for its need. Every farm animal knows how to go about its business in order to live and grow and reproduce after its kind. So do plants."

"Do you believe you have as much intelligence as a grain of wheat, or a setting hen, or a bawling calf?" I asked.

He laughed a little, thought it over quietly, and said, "You mean if they know what to do, how much more do I know? But here I am without a job, and I *don't* know what to do!"

"The grain of wheat cannot say, 'I will not grow.' It can but obey its nature. The chick cannot say, 'I refuse to hatch,' for it too is bound by the laws of nature. But man is only a 'little lower than the angels,' and he also 'has dominion' over lower nature. Man has free will. He must choose. God, the great Infinite Creative Spirit, has brought us as far by instinct or blind nature as we are to go, apparently. From here on we can use the law and progress to higher and higher things, or we can refuse. In short, we can become gods or live the life of dogs. Our Father Creator has placed this wonderful possibility in our hands, but He does not force us to use it. Therein lie all our glory and all our failure and all our shame."

"You mean," the man said, "that it is up to us? Well, I want to use this possibility. I want to know what to do that is best. I want to make decisions and carry them out. Why is it then that I cannot?"

"You are holding on to your problem too tightly," I explained. "That is fear at work. You must let go, drift. Let God handle it by guiding you. Suppose you have fallen into a lake. You hit bottom; there you grab onto the roots of an old tree or a ledge of rock and cling for dear life. But in that way you wouldn't save your life. You'd drown. Let go and you'll float up to the top."

"I feel as though I were stepping off into space," he said, "when I think of trying to work outside a grocery store, which is all I've done for years. I'm nearly sixty now."

"All right," I agreed. "Step off into space! Make up your mind that God has taken hold of your hand and that as long as God has hold of your hand you can't sink or fall or go in the wrong direction. But until you really let go of that problem God cannot take hold of your hand. God never forces. Man has free will."

The man finally saw that we should not ask for a specific thing. He said: "I see. We don't know enough to ask like that. Too many things are involved. We don't really know what is good for us!"

"We do not have to know," I reminded him. "God put us here on earth and He has a responsibility toward us."

At this point the man and I set to work, knowing that where two are agreed on a thing, it shall be done. We agreed that he would be led to his perfect place, a place that would be to his liking, that he could fill happily and well, and that it would represent and permit his further growth. He used this affirmation: "God has me by the hand, leading me now to perfect peace and plenty."

May I digress a moment to explain why the affirmation was used, and why it was only a statement and not a long, drawn out begging kind of prayer? The affirmation was to be used constantly, literally hundreds of times a day as the man went about the normal business of living. This was to permeate his outer consciousness with a truth which his soul or inner consciousness already knew. When these two had agreed, then the man could speak the word, or literally give permission to his Christ Power, or Christ Mind within, to set to work to bring about his heart's desire. A long, beseeching prayer too often has but one result: to confuse the one uttering it, and to drive doubts deeper. His affirmation was a statement of a truth. It left no room for doubt or self-argument.

Nearly two months went by. The man and his wife passed through many black moments. Several times the man tried to answer his prayer himself by calling at grocery stores and asking for work. Refusals made him very unhappy. Then he would get back into harness and try the spiritual law way. A job did materialize far across town that would have taken him several hours' travel daily. He could barely have lived on what he could earn at it. Yet he would have tried it but for our talking it over and throwing it out as his own impatient idea, born of desperation and fear, and not God's idea at all. That he saw for himself, when he tested it by asking whether the job represented growth for himself.

During all this time these two good people looked for ways to serve the Lord in their neighborhood. They were amazed to find how often they were called upon in all sorts of ways. It helped them to keep calm and remain assured their need was already being met and that soon their answer would appear.

Then one day the answer came. The man called on a large firm that grows food commercially. You may say it was mere chance that the one-time grocery man happened to read an article about the handling of frozen foods and became so interested that he read everything he could find on the subject and wound up looking into the matter as a work he would like to do. I say it was guidance, just one part of the total necessary to the answering of his prayer.

In this case, every person involved was previously unknown to the man. The new job was the best and most satisfying he had ever held. It took him to a state in which he never had thought of going to live or look for work. His big surprise was in finding how much he had to give the world. He was worth a great deal more than he had ever realized. He later agreed with me that it would have been unfair of him to take a little job when he was capable of filling a larger one and that if he had not been shoved out of a little one he never would have, of his own initiative, looked for the larger job.

I am convinced that we cannot be entirely happy if we are doing a job that is far below our capacity. It is as though an inner voice keeps saying, "Shame on you! Go forth, work to your capacity and that capacity will then be increased." Why should it be otherwise? Ours is a growing universe.

Certain it is that problems are the normal thing in life. By them we grow. Each new problem is a new opportunity. Always, always, it is not the new problem that hurts or frightens us, but only *what we think about it!* Lurking in our heart are the three old fears: fear of coming to an end of life, fear of coming to the end of love, and fear that there is no law and order in the universe, that we are at the mercy of change and chaos. These fears we have inherited from the race; fears that early man accepted before he learned to reason, and before he had discovered many laws of nature with which we are all familiar today. We no longer ring church bells to ward off the demons in lightning. We think differently about lightning from what man once did. We can control thought. We can develop an attitude of welcoming each new opportunity to grow and to do so is to line up with spiritual laws that forever protect us and lead us forward, step by step, through eternity.

I am convinced of two things: first, that there simply is no problem without an answer, that the problem and the answer are parts of a whole, and that it is good and points to growth. This problem-answer combination can be compared with stair steps. The riser is the problem; the answer the platform to which it leads and which it supports, and on which we stand while getting ready for the next step up.

These steps always lead up! We are living things. Every live thing grows. Every problem is an urge to grow. It is an invitation. But having free will, we do not have to accept this invitation. If we decide to wallow in ignorance and remain for ages undeveloped in soul growth, that it seems, is our divine right.

The second fact of which I am convinced is that few people have a high enough opinion of themselves; they are better at solving problems than they realize. They can do more work and better work than they ever dream of. They are like icebergs; only one-tenth of them is visible. The other nine-tenths lie dormant in them, as nine-tenths of the berg lie beneath the water.

If people generally realized these two facts, they would find it easier to begin a program of prayer, and would be

much less likely to give up before they had really ac-
complished their hearts' desire.

I would not have true humility turn to bragging or
egotism, for that is the worst method of selling oneself
cheaply. But I would have more clear-eyed, quiet conviction that we are divinely created and that we cannot fail;
that there is no problem without an answer.

The trouble with feeling too humble, calling ourselves
worms of the dust, is that we use it as a screen to hide
from work; to do ninety per cent less than we are capable of doing. Through prayer we can so quicken the
Spirit within us that we can double or triple our efforts
and our output. It takes more than a "worm of the dust"
to build a skyscraper or carve out the kind of career that
will make other men rise up and call one blessed. Besides,
worms are so likely to be stepped upon.

There is indeed an answer to every problem. Emerson
is quite right: "The Soul's highest duty is to be of good
cheer."

But how many problems? Most people think there
are as many problems in life as there are people to experience them. At first glance it would seem to be true.
But on closer examination, there will be found but three
basic problems in all the world. These three confront all
people on earth and most of us every day.

Once these three basic problems are understood, life
presents a pleasant pattern and becomes an exciting ad-
venture. It becomes a sure thing instead of a gamble.

The things we need to solve the three basic problems
are the things for which we can pray aright and not amiss.
To understand them is to be on the road to seeing that
the solutions are there waiting.

To understand them is to know ourselves and our fellow men as well. This knowledge enables us to deal with

every problem involving people and to eliminate the confusions of life.

In these first three chapters we have discussed *how* to pray. In the next three chapters we shall discuss *when* to pray. We shall begin with the next chapter to talk about the three basic problems of life, and in so doing, we shall the better see how we can change our lives through prayer. For we shall see when to pray, and for what to pray, and we shall see, too, that prayer cannot fail.

CHAPTER FOUR

Pray in the Morning

WE HAVE BEEN DISCUSSING the *how* of prayer, stating there were three steps: to pray aright and not amiss; to pray in faith, believing; and to wait on the Lord.

We are now ready to consider the *when* of prayer and along with it we shall discuss the three fundamental needs of life, the things for which we pray. For to fulfill these is to fulfill all.

I am sure that if we knew enough about prayer we should engage in prayer without ceasing and should put such knowledge to hourly use. Life would then become such an orderly march of events toward growth that no sudden valley of despair, no sudden mountain of doubt and fear and menace ever would confront us.

But how can we find time to pray without ceasing? We have to go about the business of earning a living, keeping house, taking care of our children and families, and our community affairs. If the time to pray is all the time, how can we get anything else done? By making everything we do a prayer.

But can we? We can and we must if we are to get out of life what the great Infinite Spirit has made it possible for us to have. To pray without ceasing is to constantly commune with God, that we may know His will and do it.

To show you how you can do that and what it will mean if you do, let me tell you about a man who tried it. His experience is to me a convincing example of what we mean when we say that praying without ceasing can change one's whole life for the better. To me this story shows that we actually can, as Paul said be "transformed by the renewing of our mind."

When this man came to me he said he was "sick of life, work, family, responsibilities, everything." His thin face wore a perpetual scowl that shouted his hatred and distrust of the world. His tight mouth and the constant futile fluttering of his hands betrayed his nervousness. He was underweight and looked ill. For a long time he had suffered from stomach trouble, he said, which caused him great distress. His clothing was old and frayed. He was in debt. A series of calamities in his life had been climaxed by a notice that his services would not be needed after the first of the month. The job he had held for years would end in thirty days.

When the man came in he was smoking a cigarette. He sat down, looked around, and not seeing an ash tray, asked for one, saying, "Don't tell me not to smoke. It's the last comfort I have left, and I'm not going to give it up for anybody. The boss doesn't like it, my wife doesn't like it, and even the kids claim they don't like the smell of tobacco."

He sat puffing in defiant silence and I sat studying him, thinking: "You have legs and feet to transport you; head, hands, eyes, and tongue to serve you. You live under the most beneficent government on earth, one founded on Christian principles, and you are free to develop mind, body, and spirit as you see fit. There are Bibles, books, lectures, information and guidance all through the city, free for your asking. You have a home, a wife, children, a profession—and smoking's your only comfort!"

The man had expected me to answer his defiant remark in some manner that would give him an excuse to fight back. Silence sometimes convicts the unhappy conscience more quickly than any sharp word of rebuke could do.

He flung the cigarette aside and said, "O. K., I'm wrong!
So what!"

"I see in you such power and glory, such ability and
such capacities for growth and great good, that your
weak words amaze me," I said, "and require me to consider carefully before I say anything at all to you."

Whatever he expected me to say, it wasn't that. My
words brought him to attention, took him off the defen-
sive, and put him in an attitude of being ready to listen
and to learn. Not because they were my words; oh, no!
But because I had seen and declared the truth about him.
I refused to accept the appearance as the reality. According to appearances he was sick, emotionally unstable, and
suffering from all the ailments of body and affairs that he
had come to enumerate.

I had declared the truth, looking past appearances.
The Christ Power in me (the power which everyone has
but which few realize and fewer still have learned to use)
spoke to the Christ Mind within him, and through that
he and I had instant understanding between us.

The man enumerated his troubles. I said: "There are
not as many problems as there are hours in the day; only
one, and that is the problem of how to live as God intended you should and to get out of life what you need.
Your wants are few; they are three. If they are satisfied
there is no problem. If not, the want, need, or desire becomes a problem until it is fulfilled. In other words, it is
somewhat like an order, and remains on the order sheet
until it has been filled."

"But I need everything," the man persisted. "A new
job, clothes, better health, money. I need self-confidence,
too. I even need a better disposition. Quarrel with everybody. I'm ashamed when I see my wife and children unhappy, but I'm unhappy, too!—failing, falling behind,
being a nobody."

"You have listed the three things we all have need of," I said. "They are the things we truly want. We get side-tracked with the thousands of little calls on our time and energy, but if we traced each of them back to its source we should find that each of them grew out of one or more of our three fundamental needs. These three are: the need to keep on living, the need to be happy with our fellow creatures, and the need to progress, or grow. In simpler words, God gave us the urge to live, to love, and to learn."

The man did not accept this at first, so we went into it a little more fully about as follows:

Every human being has the urge to live, that is, to keep alive the spark of his own individual self. To this end he struggles for food, clothing, shelter, and most of all, a job, for a job means money to secure these other needs. He strives for good health, and in the end he hopes for life after death.

But just to live is not enough. No, not even to be assured of life after death. So we have the second urge, to love and to reproduce after our kind. Along with it, never separated from it, is the all-powerful urge to protect and keep the life-spark burning in our offspring.

However, just to keep our own life-spark burning, to reproduce after our kind, and to keep the life-spark burning in these new creatures is not enough for the experience we call life on earth. No, love is not enough. Not even when we consider the ultimate of love, which is to be assured that God approves us, just as we want our own parents, our children, and our loved ones to approve us. Neither life nor love is the ultimate purpose of our journey here on earth. There is that third urge, the last, for which the first two were made. There is learning or wisdom.

The purpose of all life is growth. We live, we love,

in order to grow, to know, to do, to be. The ultimate of wisdom which we are all seeking, whether we are conscious of it or not, is to find God, to know the whole story of man. It is this urge at work when we seek Truth, or final knowledge of all there is, which is another way of saying seek to find God and to know man's relation to him, and the plan for man. It is this last urge which has led us to religion, philosophy, and science. It has also led us to the arts. To seek beauty is also to try to fit the parts to the whole, a task in which man has been employed since time began.

After considerable explaining, the man felt he could accept the idea that since the Infinite Spirit which had created us had implanted those desires in us, they had been given for a very definite purpose. He also agreed, since these urges had to do with the ultimate of man, that man would be inwardly stirred to fulfill those desires; that he would be presented with situations which would require him to struggle in order to fulfill those desires.

After we had come to that agreement, it was not far to concluding that, since it meant so much to the Power that created us to have us satisfy those desires, it also stood to reason that there was no chance of failing if we would but try! But also, since we are creatures of free will, that there was no force in the matter, and that it was up to man first to be willing for God to step in and help. For to have help forced upon us would of necessity rob us of our free will. We should then be no higher in the scheme of things than vegetables or the lower animals.

The man next agreed that our only real problem was how to communicate with God, this Father who created us; how to draw near and receive guidance and encouragement. "But," he wailed, "how can I do that?"

"Through prayer," I said. "There is no answer but prayer."

"Never said a prayer in my life," he muttered. "Don't know how to beg God for things."

"You do not have to beg," I assured him. "You have only to see how much you have to be grateful for and to give thanks. To give thanks without ceasing is to pray without ceasing. It is to bring our consciousness to the God consciousness where a meeting can take place. After that we see what to do. We can give thanks again, speak the word, do the act, and see the result."

That is how we began. We spent the morning talking about prayer without ceasing, and in his case, about thanking God without ceasing. To simplify his problem we broke up the day into three parts. I said something like this:

"When you first wake up in the morning, instead of hating to get up, hating to take that first cold step, turn your thoughts to God and think along these lines: 'During the night, while I slept, God kept my heart beating, my lungs breathing, my blood circulating. This was done through spiritual laws that God has established and that man cannot break nor need be concerned about. Through the night I was safe. Blessed was the night. Now I arise and give thanks. Blessed be the morning to me and to mine.' "

Once out of bed, instead of dreading the morning shower and shaving, this man was to go on giving thanks and blessing the morning and every task and opportunity it held. Under the shower he was to think something like this:

"God working in the hearts and minds of man has created this comfort for me. Water is brought to my home, heated, and now plays upon my body for my comfort and benefit. This water is the symbol of a power that washes away all previous mistakes, worry and un-happiness. My heart is singing in the shower, for I am being bathed in the warm love of God, of which the warm water is a symbol. I give thanks for this blessing. Blessed be the morning to me and mine."

Shaving had become such a task that in an angry, defi-ant spirit this man had of late occasionally gone to the office unshaved. He was instructed to think along these lines as he shaved:

"This electric razor is another proof of God's love and infinite creative power. It is a proof of the law of progressive good that forever carries man forward. There are certain spiritual laws under which the universe operates. Man has been a long time learning these laws and a long time learning how to make contact with God, but whenever one such law is discovered and put to use, great benefits and pleasures result for all men who will make use of them.

"The electricity that operates this razor is still a mys-tery to man. We know how to use it, but we don't yet know what it is. It is a powerful force. But it is not so powerful as thought. It can be controlled by man through his thoughts and acts. I can think. Therefore I have within me a power greater than that of electricity. Electricity is my servant. My prayers are servants, too. I send them forth. My word does not return unto me void. It accomplishes that whereunto I send it. Blessed be the morning to me and to mine."

The next hurdle in that man's day was the breakfast hour. Lately he had worked himself into such a state that he was certain before he sat down to eat that the food was not going to agree with him. His family had let his worries and scolding become such a part of their life that breakfast was a hurried, unhappy time for all. The mother said later, "I was cooking unhappiness and inharmony into their food and ironing it into their clothes."

The man was instructed to forget himself at breakfast and to visit with his wife and children and to instruct the children in lessons of gratitude for the food and for all other blessings that they enjoyed. For example, he was to tell them about the mystery of a grain of wheat becoming a hot cereal and toast on the table; of the laws of God working in the sunshine, the rain, and the soil; of the people who had made it possible for them to have a breakfast—the planter, the harvester, the baker, the storekeeper—and to point out that all these people were God's people.

When we had settled on how to pray during the breakfast hour, we went on to the next step: leaving the house in prayer. The man had never before realized what he was doing to himself, his wife and his two children by slamming the door when he left home every morning, irritated, scolding, and hurrying.

"The way to leave your house in prayer," I said, "is to be conscious of your blessings and thankful for them. Remember you have a duty toward your children in getting them started right for the day. Jesus, the Way-Shower, blessed the children. So must you. To arouse fear or weeping resentment in them, to start them off to school in a state of fear and unhappiness, is to handicap them for the day, and if persisted in, will harm their health. You must consciously try to make their paths peaceful. It is not enough for you to earn their bread. We do not live by bread alone; we live by love and hope and happiness, also. It is under these that we grow. And these cost nothing but the willingness to give.

"Instead of going out like a crashing thunderstorm, leave your home as a man of God should—in dignity, poise and peace. Leave your loved ones with your praises

and good wishes for them ringing in their ears. Let them
know you love them. Let them think of you as happy to
work for them. Think of yourself as a servant of the
Lord doing good works, and give thanks for the opportunity."

After we had gone into the problems of this initial
part of his morning, we took up the next difficulty, which
was connected with his going to work. The man sometimes drove to work; this was in the days before rationing; but the car was old and "something was always happening to it," so he "just hated to get the old wreck out
of the garage." On the other hand, when he went by
street-car he suffered even more.

Remember, this man had said he "hated the world,
especially the people in it, and more especially those who
rode on the street-cars." Everything was wrong with
those people. Everything about them irritated him—their
clothes, their gum-chewing, their talk, everything. He felt
the thumping of the wheels going through his body, just
as every stop signal ground through his body.

This, let me explain, is not an unusual or exaggerated
case of the average business man of today, laboring with
what he says are too little money and too many problems
—and what is true of business men is true of housewives,
too. Small wonder that heart trouble has become the
killer that it has.

The man in our story was told to drop the worry and
to let the forces of God's all-pervading good ideas possess him on the way to work. If he drove his car, he was
to drive more slowly than usual and to use the stop sig-
nals for periods of thanks. The sign was there to protect
him. He was to see something and name something for
which he was thankful every time he stopped his car.

If he rode in the street-car he was to relax and to bless
the people around him. He was to think something like

this: "All the good ideas that benefit mankind today were brought to earth through the minds of men. Most of them were answers to prayers. Perhaps someone in this car is now working out some problem, getting an answer from God, the source of all there is, and I will give him my aid, which costs me nothing but willingness, my silent blessing. God bless this car and all who are in it. Blessed be the morning to them and their loved ones."

When on the point of arriving at his destination he was not to get up and stand, swaying, tense, a full block before his stop, but to sit quietly, thanking God that he had time in which to do everything that needed to be done, time in which to think every thought that needed consideration, and an eternity in which to work out his God-given task.

At his desk he would then be ready for the next portion of his day, for which, "Work while you pray and pray while you work," seemed the appropriate directive. This point we shall take up in our next chapter. Here let us consider you and your problems of the morning, which may run parallel to those of the man in our story.

It makes no difference what you are, business man, housewife, teacher, or defense worker; the problems for all of us are the same. We all desire the same three things. We all desire to maintain life and to do so we must have food, clothing and shelter. For these we want a job and a home. We all desire the blessings of love. We want to give to our loved ones; we want their approval, companionship, admiration, and we want the ability to get along well with others, and to be thought well of by them. In our secret hearts we want to follow God's directions, for we instinctively know that to do so is to reach our highest goal. The unhappy thing is that we so often do not know how, or worse yet, that we neglect to try.

Certainly the people around us have the same desire for power that we have, for all men are brothers. We desire the ability to learn, to progress, to go forward instead of back, with our experiences in life. We all seek Reality, or God, the ultimate for man.

Learning to pray keeps us in tune all the time. When we forget to count our blessings and turn away from God, we forget that all men are brothers, and we are soon in trouble. Our money always comes through channels of others. How important it is to know how to fully appreciate our fellow men. How important to turn to God for all wisdom. There can be no lasting success or happiness without divine guidance. Solomon was a wise man. He was a rich man. He never asked God for riches but for wisdom. Others came to him because of his wisdom, which he had received from God, and gladly gave him money for it.

The man in our story learned the value, the absolute necessity, of praying without ceasing as a means of changing his life and affairs. He learned to go from saying: "Blessed be the morning to me and mine," which is a prayer of petition or asking, to saying, "Blessed *is* the morning to me and mine!" That is a prayer of acceptance and declaration, a thanksgiving for the truth about life.

The principles that the man of our story applied to his problems you can apply to yours. You need not wait to see how much more he learned or how he came out with the program of praying without ceasing. You can start now by declaring "Blessed be the morning to me and mine." You can start today to pray while you work; and this very night you can begin to pray while you rest.

CHAPTER FIVE

Pray While You Work

WE ARE TRYING to learn how to make life one constant experience of harmony, happiness and growth—how to make it, as the poet expressed it, "One grand sweet song." For with some inner knowledge which we seldom, if ever, stop to examine, we all know that life could be better than it ever has been for the whole of humanity. And we are, as individuals, constantly urged from within to work toward that ideal, to make our outer lives as wonderful as our inner dreams.

In the first three chapters we discussed the method of prayer which would enable us to make our earth "as it is in heaven." We said we must learn how to pray aright, to pray in faith, believing, and having prayed, to wait on the Lord for the answer. Waiting on the Lord also means to become a servant unto Him. We serve the Lord when we serve our fellow men and when we do good works. Actually, every serious thought and every earnest attempt to know and to do the will of the Lord, is service unto Him.

How often ought we to pray? Shall we wait until some big problem confronts us, or shall we decide once and for all, to learn to pray without ceasing, so that life will become a constant demonstration of good and growth, without sudden intervals of fear and despair?

To show how we can change our whole lives and affairs from sickness, poverty, and unhappiness, to health, sufficiency, plenty, and happiness by praying without ceasing, we discussed the experience of a man who tried this method.

As we go into this man's problem again, let us remember he was not trying to solve one specific problem after another, though apparently that is what he needed to do. What he wanted was a whole, full, and happy life. He wanted to maintain life, because that is a part of God's plan for all men. He wanted more happiness in his family life. He wanted self-respect. He wanted his wife and children to respect him. He was unhappy in his work, in his home, and in his own secret heart. He wanted to develop a sense of power, and to "get ahead."

This man's problem was the problem we all face. Every intelligent man at some time asks himself who he is, how he got there, why he came, and where he is going when he dies; whether death is real and whether he is a puppet or a man of free will. On the answers that he finds and accepts depend his health, wealth, and happiness.

The man in our story never had learned how to pray and said he could not "beg God." He was advised to thank God instead, and was given a program of praying without ceasing. He began by learning to pray in the morning, taking "Blessed be the morning to me and mine" as his affirmation. This, we said, would help him turn back to God, the Creator of all; help him to arise from his lowly state and return unto the Father. For prayer always is a lifting-up process and begins to prove so, long before we have become very proficient in praying.

When the man had learned to bless the morning it was not so hard to go on to the next step, which was to pray while he worked.

"When you learn to pray as you work you will work joyously and restingly. We can put forth twice as much energy in doing a thing we want to do as we can in doing something we dislike. We can be highly stimulated by the former and tired out by the latter," I said.

"That's my case," the man sighed. "I hate my work from the time I sit down at the desk until I get up to go home. If I had another job to go to when the month is up, I'd be glad I am losing this one."

"One of two things is wrong," I said. "Praying while you work will reveal which is wrong and can heal either of them. Either you have the wrong attitude about a work that is rightfully yours and that you can learn to enjoy doing, or it is the wrong job for you. That is, you are either too little or too big for your job."

"I don't see how I can find out," he worried.

"By praying while you work. By blessing every minute of your working time. By making up your mind there is a right place for you and one that you can happily fill. All good work is holy. There is a right place for every good worker. Bless the books you keep, the boy who brings your ink supply; especially bless the boss you have hated. Every vacant minute say, 'My work is a prayer for good for me and mine.' That is why you work, isn't it? To earn money with which to buy things for your family and yourself. Put prayer into it and watch it return blessings to you, crammed down and running over."

Again and again the man was told that the very act of praying, the very desire to come into communion with reality, with God, is in itself a form of faith that there is Something that hears and answers prayer. Prayer always is a form of arising from whatever unwanted and unhappy condition the petitioner finds himself in and making at least a start toward the happy condition he desires. Thus, when prayer is practiced enough, it is as though scales fall from the eyes. Facts before overlooked now become significant. People, places, and things take on a new aspect. This is because prayer makes us a channel through which new good can flow. Not even one sincere desire to find God ever goes unrewarded. We have but to put the wilful self aside. This is allowing "Thy will be done" in reality and is not just a parrot-like repetition of words.

That is what the man discovered. The first day's attempt to pray without ceasing got off to a good start at home. He left in a happier mood than he had experienced in a long time. He was not so successful in controlling his feelings on the street-car. But the very fact that he kept on trying cleared his vision.

As soon as he was settled at his desk he started to light a cigarette, which his "boss hated so." He had an impulse to look up. The boss, a non-smoker and manager of the department, was glaring at him angrily. He put the cigarette aside and went on with his work. He said, later, that it never had occurred to him before that taking time out to smoke on the job was actually stealing from the company. For the first time he realized that his boss did not object to the smoking, but to the fact that it was done on company time. "I would not have taken a penny from the company till," the man said. "I would not have carried home a three-cent stamp from my desk. I thought of myself as absolutely honest. Being a bookkeeper, I computed the probable time I had stolen through indulging in smoking on the job. I was appalled at the figure. I saw I had been hating the boss without reason."

The man did not feel the need of smoking again that morning. Formerly, in these interludes of smoking, he had poured out bitter thoughts about his boss, his work, everything and anything that annoyed him. But having caught the picture of thoughts as living things of form and color and substance, he said he knew at last what it meant to have the air "tense with feeling." He was learning to fill in vacant moments with prayers. Of course, the atmosphere cleared and became pleasant.

The man had formerly disliked eating at noon in the cafeteria maintained by the company for the employees. But this day of prayer had so far opened his eyes that he decided to analyze his feeling and see just why he hated to eat there. The food was excellent. It cost him less than eating outside did.

After some quiet and honest thinking he discovered that he hated to eat there because it made him feel poor! He saved money by eating there, and instead of seeing that this was a blessing and thanking God for it, as for all blessings, he had turned it into a curse. He could not afford to eat out often. He wanted to feel rich and important. He had come to dislike the cafeteria so heartily that his lunches there more often than not disagreed with him.

"Yes, first you made the poison, then you ate it!" I pointed out to him. "When we forget to be thankful we are very soon cooking up and eating trouble. Food without prayer can easily become poison and it most certainly does when we think poisonous thoughts about it."

To continue with his problem: All that day the man went on with his thanks and acknowledgment of blessings. At quitting time his boss sent for him and told him he would be let out in two weeks instead of at the end of the month.

The old panic, the old fear took hold of the man. He came to me white and shaking. What should he do now?

"That's what you've been praying for," I reminded him. "You want a job more to your liking. Perhaps the old one was too little for you. We never are happy unless we are doing somewhere near our best."

"But what is my best? What can I turn to now? Expenses will go on. We still need food to live."

"You have two more weeks," I replied, "in which to pray without ceasing—pray in the morning, pray while you work, and pray while you rest."

We talked at length again about how our heavenly Father must surely want us to live; about the desires planted in our hearts, so that we should make an effort to fulfil them. We talked about Jesus' promises, that He had said anyone of us could do what He had done if we would learn the laws—obey the Father.

"Jesus taught the creative power of every man's word and thought," I said. "He explained also the law of forgiveness. 'Neither do I condemn thee; go and sin no more.' We do not have to keep on and on paying for a mistake made last year or yesterday. Do not think your losing this job is some kind of punishment meted out for some past mistake. All you have to do to wipe out a past mistake is to call on the law of forgiveness and avoid repeating the mistake. It will then be remembered no more against you."

The man admitted that part of his fear had been a sense of guilt and of deserving punishment. But after considerable talking it through he reached the point where he could agree that if enough people throughout the world lived their daily lives according to Christian precepts it would change the affairs of all men. For it would make of all men brothers without jealousies, fears, or desire for punishment and revenge among them. In a final burst of insight and enthusiasm he said, "It is so simple! It is so profound! It will yet revolutionize human conduct!"

It was a short step from his seeing this truth to seeing that he, individually, need not wait for the world to catch up, that as an individual he could revolutionize his own life here and now.

He began getting up one hour earlier every morning

to read the Bible. Again and again he went over Jesus' promises, trying to understand the meaning in them. He found that to seek was to find, to knock was to have the door of Truth opened unto him. The more Truth he saw the more he was "set free," and the more diligently he sought. This became an unbreakable circle; it was fast becoming an unshakable faith, which is what happens when one truly tries. "It is as though I have never really used my mind before; never actually saw people or facts before," said the man in amazement.

The more the man repeated his affirmation, "My work is a prayer for me and mine," the more he realized the blessings of work. It could not have been otherwise. Prayers such as his could no more produce curses than fig trees can produce thistles. Every word, every belief, produces after its kind. Soon the man was seeing all honest work as prayer.

Next, the man saw that his work not only blessed himself but others, in an ever widening circle. He saw that he was, he must be, a servant unto the Lord; that the unknown hundreds whom his work affected had a holy right to expect his work to be a prayer. He saw himself as the answer to others' prayers. He began to think of himself as needed and wanted, even though no one put the fact into words to him. He began slowly to see that the problem of employment was not his, so much as it was God's.

There was another part of his program of praying while he worked that required attention outside working hours. This was scattering the blessings that he had received from work. He learned to bless money, to bless every coin that came to his hand and every coin that left it. He learned not to complain about high prices or scarcity of things he wanted, seeing it was a waste of time and energy. Complaints do not right evils. Prayers that lead to right acts do.

In trying to think what kind of new job he would like, the man began with the right idea: that all honest work is prayer. Work that does not bless all is not prayer and if it is performed by a person who hopes to get a blessing out of it for himself at the expense of others, it is dealing in evils and not in blessings, and the person will himself be harmed by the very things he sets in motion with the idea of blessing himself and harming others. This is spiritual law and is so well known to the people of all ages that we find it running in all literature and history. In today's modern short-short stories it forms the theme of most of them—the biter that gets bitten.

Later, in pursuit of his program, the man learned to pray while resting. Still later he discovered that all rest is a prayer of gratitude, and that if rest is not a prayer of thanksgiving it is not rest but some miscreated evil that will in turn have to be righted before real rest can come.

Before we go into the balance of the man's story, let us here consider you and how you can pray while you work. If you fail to pray while you work you are throwing away some of the best hours of your life that might be used to bring you the secret desires of your heart. Normally, we work some eight hours a day. Housewives, farmers, and others work many more hours than that. All have a splendid chance to change their lives by praying while they work.

Do you like your work? Is it fun or drudgery? Is it a prayer? If you are too big or too little, a misfit in your job, start this prayer program and see things change for the better. Use the affirmation the man in the story used, "My work is a prayer for good for me and mine," and see what miracles it can work in your life.

How about the people with whom you work? Do they annoy you? Do they belittle your efforts, and are they below the standard you would set for those around you? Learn to pray while you work. You will then begin to be the kind of person you would like to have around you. You will grow more inwardly calm, more outwardly poised. You will see others in a different light; and do not doubt it, they will see you differently also. You can grow out of the place that you are too big to fill; you can promote yourself to better surroundings. Like attracts like; change yourself and you change your circumstances and hence those around you.

Among the people who complain to me that their job is a thankless one, housewives hold the record. The trouble is not in the work itself but in the way they look at it. They fail to put prayer into their work. The man who said "God could not be everywhere and so He made mothers," had an appreciation of truth much beyond the average.

There is no job in art or science, in politics or commerce, in any activity in which man is today engaged in order to earn a living, that would not be better done if prayer were put into it.

Ever since Jesus Christ came to earth to show men how to live there have been at least some people in every age who believed that His teachings could solve the ills of mankind. Now people are coming to see more than ever that He did indeed come to fulfill the law and not to destroy it. Now, while this movement is on, while men everywhere are thinking along these lines, is the time for all of us to learn to pray without ceasing. For we shall get an added benefit from the collective or race thoughts going on all about us.

Then let us arise and bless the morning, pray while we work and pray while we rest, as our individual contribution to the total effort now being made to make our world a better place in which to live. Let us through prayer help ourselves and our fellow men toward that better life of which we all are inwardly aware. Let us make the without as the within.

In our next chapter we shall talk about how to pray while we rest.

CHAPTER SIX

Pray While You Rest

WE HAVE DISCUSSED *how* to pray and have said that the *when* of prayer is all the time; that it is the praying without ceasing which changes lives and conditions from what they are to what we want them to be. We see why this is necessarily true when we consider that prayer is a *conscious* desire and effort to know God. For it then follows that the more often we are conscious of God, or a law of all good, all love, all wisdom, and all growth, the more likely we are to live our lives in accordance with God's plan for man.

We have seen the value of starting the day with prayer, giving thanks, and using the affirmation, "Blessed be the morning for me and mine." We have talked about praying while we work and of making our very work a prayer. For any one can make his work a prayer just as surely as he can make his prayers work. Now, let us consider the possibilities of praying while we rest.

Of all the times of the day in which we are really free to give ourselves up to prayer, a rest period in the evening or at night would seem to be the best. Of course, any rest period can be used, but there is something about the coming of the night that is conducive to prayer. There is a recess in the hurry and work of the day, a leisure period to devote to reading, music, walking under the stars, a period in which to contemplate life, the universe around us, and the great Infinite Spirit which is God, and man's place in the scheme of things.

Not to use at least a portion of this period for prayer is to throw away one of our best opportunities to enrich life, to increase the output of whatever work we may be doing and to attune ourselves to harmony, joy, and peace instead of forever vibrating to the thoughts of drudgery and worry.

In the hope that it will help in following a program of praying while we rest, I want to tell you more of the experiences of the man who tried such a plan. You will remember he was "tired of life, family, responsibilities, everything." He "hated his work and people; quarreled with everyone." To all appearance he was sick; he was in debt. He had been notified that he was no longer needed in the office where he had worked for several years.

Having experienced a startling change in his home life by blessing his morning and seeing that his own words and acts were in accordance with the idea that the morning is blessed, he was the more encouraged to pray while he worked. So he prayed, giving thanks for his rich blessings, even though he knew that his job would last only two more weeks.

The hardest thing for him was to learn to pray while resting. He had been a highly nervous man, "keyed up yet craving excitement at the end of the workday," he explained. This had proved expensive, whether he went out alone or took his wife. If he went alone he "always was unhappy and generally ended up having a few drinks."

I said something like this to him: "Your mad chase after excitement is really an attempt to run away from yourself. You have been living an outward life of which your inner life or soul does not approve. Your outer conscience cannot bear the silent accusations of your soul, for your soul always is in communion with God the Father. The life you have been living is so far below the level of your capacities and your inner desires, that for a long time now you have hated your work, thought of yourself as a failure, and have been trying to excuse yourself. Stop running. Stop failing. Stand still and conquer."

"You are more right than you know," the man admitted sadly.

I talked to him at length about his rightful heritage; that he, being a creature of the most high God, the Creator of the universe, was a Prince of Earth, and that he ought to conduct himself as such. He had been given dominion over all the earth, including dominion over his own thoughts; that such dominion meant "the right of absolute possession and use; ownership," and that he had been using this tremendous power to his own harm instead of to his help. For that reason he was inwardly ashamed, and was therefore running, trying to hide from himself, because he knew he alone was at fault, no matter how much he might try to place the blame on others or on circumstances.

(Just in passing, I want to state that I have never worked with an alcoholic who was not running from himself; that is, "covering up" for some reason or other. The reasons were many and varied. The healing took place when the alcoholic faced the truth about himself, and learned the truth about his true station in life and his relationship with God.)

To go on with our man in the story: We talked about rest and how to pray while resting. I did not mean that he was to go home from work, get down on his knees in a dark closet and pray until dinner time, then go back and pray until bedtime, then pray till he fell asleep. No; but I did mean for him to be conscious of God and so of his real self *all the while*. He was to start saying, "Blessed be the evening for me and mine," as soon as he left the office for home.

The man had been accustomed to reading the evening papers on the way home, and his impulse was to take on every worry and threat the headlines suggested. By the time he reached home he was he said "fit to be tied," because he had accepted the race fears and had forgotten God.

Following instructions, he did not read while riding home that day but spent the time thinking up some surprise, some way to make his family happy that night. He arrived in a calm state of mind but still without a plan. Following instructions, he did not turn on the radio after dinner. His youngest child timidly approached him and said:

"You look very unbusy, Daddy. Tell me a story as good as the one you told at breakfast about the farmer in blue overalls that planted our toast only it was just wheat then and not even flour yet."

The man said to me, later: "I saw my child that night for the first time. I saw her looking to me very much as I might look to God. I saw that I must indeed serve her if I was to expect God to serve me. I realized, with a pain of regret, that so far I had failed her in many ways in which I should have served."

He surprised the child by saying, "All right, I'll tell you another story. This one is about a wood-cutter who wore a red checked shirt and high leather boots. He lived in the woods." He told her the story of the table on which their lamp stood. He surprised his wife by his knowledge of wood, lumber, and manufacturing. Most of all, he pleasantly surprised himself with the joy he had in talking about something he really liked. In high school, years before, he had enjoyed shop work. He had always wanted a shop of his own some day—when they had a larger house, a better place to put a shop, more money with which to buy equipment. He had always wanted to make things.

When we talked it over I said, "Now is the accepted time to act on these good desires. Start work tonight with your hands, and pray while you work. Pray to be shown what God wants you to do with your head and heart and hands. Use what you have in the way of equipment and knowledge and more will be added unto you. It is a spiritual law of supply that the more we use the more will come to us. This is the lesson Jesus taught in the parable of the talents. Do not bury your talent. Use it."

The man made a box to hold the youngest child's toys, made it from scrap material with a pocket knife, a hammer, and some nails. The other child at once wanted things for his room, too. Several happy evenings were spent in the kitchen, making things.

During these several evenings the man got no further with his prayer program than just saying to himself and trying to feel that it was true: "Blessed is the evening for me and mine." For he had come to accept it as such and no longer asked it to be blessed; he simply and fully accepted it as true, "whether I can see it all the time or not," as he said.

Then one night at dinner he remarked to his wife, "You are a very good cook. I wonder why I haven't noticed it before. Your food tastes so much better than any I can get downtown."

No sooner had he said it than he "became aware all at once of the clean tablecloth, the nicely ironed napkins, the gleaming silver—evidence on every hand of his wife's love and desire to please him."

Till now the man had taken these simple blessings for granted. He had shut himself off from them by remaining indifferent or blind to them. Through his program

of prayer he was fast becoming aware of many joys that
he had not known before. He realized how much his
wife's love and devotion meant to him; how much it
meant to have two starry-eyed children waiting for him
to come home. He began to wonder that night just how
much he had been missing through his own wilful blind-
ness.

The thought followed him to bed. He thought of how
his wife had washed and ironed the sheets, how the sun
had dried his washed clothes, how all life was a "working proposition from beginning to end." He began to see
that rest was good after a good day's work.

Lying in the stillness and dark of the night, the man
thought about the wool in the blankets that covered him.
Some shepherd had tended the sheep. The thought led
him back to his childhood, to Sunday-school, to thoughts
of Jesus the Good Shepherd.

"I was never before so aware of how closely the world
is knit together," he afterwards told me. "I never before
saw the importance of the individual to the whole scheme
of things. Now I understand what you mean about waiting on the Lord, and how necessary it is that we do so.
I see that God must have had need of me or He wouldn't
have put me here."

You see what that man was doing? By giving thanks,
by drawing closer to God, which he did through the process of purposeful thinking, he was being quickened in
perception and reflection, and was on the way to learning
how to ask and how to receive. But, as it is with all of
us, *his* had to be the first step.

As the days went by he kept up his program of praying; and he began to gain weight, to improve in health
and in nerves. He decided that smoking for him was
silly and extravagant and gave it up. "It was such a
personal, selfish thing in which I indulged, using money

that might better have been spent on things I could share with my family," he explained.

Then one night, as he took the family for a little walk before bedtime, a pastime which gave them all pleasure, an idea came to him. He knew what he wanted to do. He did not know where the idea had come from he said; he just accepted the fact that since he had been praying he had "somehow opened up something that before was closed," and he saw clearly what he had not seen before.

The next day he made arrangements to take night school training in the thing he wanted to do. He did it in spite of the fact that he did not then know where the money for tuition was coming from, or the money to live on until he got another daytime job.

He said: "I am willing to work hard and with all the intelligence and loyalty I have. God knows where the job is that I am needed to fill. I am willing to be a servant unto Him. I'll be led to that job." He knew it so certainly that he did not even try to find it as long as he was on the other job. He did not want to slight that job in order to look for another.

Of course, he was led to the new job. It was in line with the training he had already decided upon. The work for which he had prayed in secret, in silence, through his hopes, his desire, and his willingness, was offered to him openly. He accepted the new job not alone as a means of earning a living. He accepted it as a way of serving the Lord by working to his highest capacity to serve his employer and his fellow men.

The man did not stop his program of praying without ceasing. He learned to keep sunny, no matter how hard it rained. He learned to keep his faith in God and in the right working out of human affairs, regardless of newspaper headlines. If a neighbor came in filled with fear and penny-dreadful politics, or race hatreds, he did not let it upset him. Instead, he let it make him more conscious of the fact that Christian principles are the hope of the world; that they must be put into effect as a means of saving mankind from their own ignorance and folly. And, quite rightly, he saw that his duty was not to reform the world but to reform himself.

The man learned to live simply and to think constructively. He stopped running from himself. He found he neither needed nor wanted many of his former recreations, seeing them to be conducive not to rest but to unrest and a source of new problems. People were no longer an annoyance to him. When he looked at their unhappy and fear-filled faces he had compassion on them without taking on any of their error-laden thoughts. He learned to go about silently blessing all with whom he came in contact, so that his very presence became a healing power. He looked for good in everyone and, of course, never failed to find some good about which he could speak.

From being quarrelsome, which drove people from him, he became a center to which people gravitated. They came to be warmed by the fires of brotherly love that now burned in his inner life so that they cast warmth and light in his outer life. This man was on the way to knowing what Jesus really meant by saying His yoke was easy and His burden light.

The man took an interest in his children's school activities, in the problems of his neighbors, in his community. He learned to listen to the voice of nature and to see God and to feel His presence everywhere. "I see new beauties every day," he once reported to me. "I have never before been aware of the great need of beauty in our everyday lives." He learned to find beauty in the acts and thoughts of others. Slowly he came to see that there is no peace, safety, happiness, or worth while reason for living, outside the laws of God; that the highest

use which man can make of his free will is to use it diligently to find God and to know His will.

By continuing his program of prayer the man reached
a high level of faith where he knew beyond any doubt
that nothing could hurt him. To him the ninety-first
Psalm was utter truth. No matter what the threat or
fear, it would not come nigh him. He knew that he was
a child of God, that his soul would never die, and that
though his human body might be destroyed, he, the real
living self, could never be hurt.

"I never again will try to live without constant prayer,"
he said. "To attempt to do so is deliberately walking out
of the safe and lighted path into the deepest, darkest
jungle of night."

Constant prayer keeps us conscious of eternity in relation to our little individual lifetime and helps us to act
accordingly. Let us consider this for a moment:

We all want a better world. We all want more truth,
beauty, justice, and freedom for ourselves and for others.
We want to fulfill our desires to live, love, and learn.
Now we see that they must come for all men of all
nations, if they are to be guaranteed for any man. How
are we to supply all these needs?

First, let us ask ourselves why we want all these things.
Why are we not satisfied with things as they are? Who
has told us there is a better way of living than man ever
has tried? What is it in man that forever drives or leads
him to do all he can to make life easier, pleasanter, and
happier for himself and his children, to make the world
better than the world he inherited?

We know the answer, do we not? At least, we know
it when we take time to consider as we do when we pray.
This is man in search of God. Jesus taught us to pray
"Thy will be done in earth as it is in heaven." In plain
words, we are told that it is quite possible to make the

without the same as the *within*. We can make our dreams come true! We can realize our visions. We can make our world of actuality as beautiful, wonderful, safe, harmonious, and happy as our inner dreams! For the truth is, we could not dream about them, could not desire them, if it were not also possible to fulfill those dreams. Our urges are God's invitation to growth.

All growth is from within. Here we get our messages from our Father, God. Here, to the very center of our being, comes God to inspire, lead, guide, and invite us on our onward march. But never to force us. If we listened to these inner teachings only, and discounted all appearances to the contrary in the outer world, we should march much faster and surer. This is where prayer comes in. Prayer is *conscious* desire to listen to God.

When we do as well as we know, produce as well as we dream, act as well as we think, we shall be able to have the kingdom on earth as it is in heaven. It is from within that we build and plan a new world. A bright day will dawn on the world when enough people make a conscious effort to make contact with their invisible powers —which is to say, with God—and then act on the ideas received. That day is not so far away as some may think.

You can help bring that day nearer by praying without ceasing. After the day's work is done, rest and think of yourself as resting in the arms of the Lord. When night comes, thank God for it, for the rest it brings. Believe in this Infinite Spirit around you, have faith in it, call upon it. It will never disappoint you if you trust in it.

Use some of your rest hours for letting go all inhibitions, all reserves, and imagine yourself talking to and working with God to build a better life for yourself and a better world for all mankind. It will help you if you think of God as a wise, all-loving Father with whom you can counsel as you would with an earthly father. Some-

times learning along certain lines raises so many questions that faith is pushed aside. Throw aside such questions of learning. Become as a little child. The late
Doctor Carver used the childlike approach in discovering
the many uses for the lowly peanut. He has given us an
account of how he walked in the fields and woods and
asked God what He wanted him to do that day.

Whatever your problem, whatever your desire, take
it to the Lord in prayer. There the answer awaits you.
Make your prayer in the stillness of the night and God
will answer in the heat and work of the day. When you
have made your prayer, use *Psalms,* sixth chapter, ninth
verse, which reads as follows: "The Lord hath heard my
supplication; the Lord will receive my prayer," and know
in your heart the answer will be forthcoming. So, rest
in the Lord.

This chapter closes the first two divisions of the book
which were *how* to pray and *when* to pray. The first six
chapters covered the theory of prayer and gave examples
of how others have used prayer to change their lives. We
are now ready to discuss your particular problem more
fully. Before going into that, in the next chapter, I wish
at this junction of our study to make a definite promise
to the reader concerning prayer.

My promise is this:

If you will truly learn *how* to pray, *when* to pray and
what to pray for, and will then honestly live by a prayer
program, you will be born anew. You will be able to
double, triple, your effort and output in your work. You
will understand people and their motives, so that they
never again can hurt you. You will find yourself above
both praise and blame. You never again will fear anything as long as you live. You will find peace that "pass-
eth understanding," and that surpasses mere happiness
and joy. You will find your rightful place in life and

more satisfaction in living than you have before thought possible.

A very large promise? A sweeping statement? Try it for yourself. Remember, prayer is *conscious desire* and *attempt* to find and worship (willingly work with) the great Infinite Spirit of the universe, Father and God of all men and of all time. To succeed in that attempt, even once, is to find that "all things are become new." To be able to repeat the experience at will is to find heaven on earth.

CHAPTER SEVEN

Praying for Wealth

IF YOU SHOULD WALK into my office today and ask for help, you would find, after analysis of your problem, that it had grown out of one or more of the three desires which are common to all men: the desire for more of life, of love, or of learning. In the final analysis this is the great hunger for more "livingness"; that is, the great desire to be *more alive*. I borrow that word from Thomas Troward, for it so precisely expresses this desire which God has given us.

Since most people think that if they only had money enough, or more money, they could either solve all the other problems of life or cheerfully leave them unsolved, we shall talk about wealth first. For wealth, of course, means a supply of food, clothing, and shelter, needed to keep the life-spark burning within us. It is a symbol of health in the minds of most people. There are many who believe that wealth can also buy love and wisdom. The truth is that wealth cannot even give love or wisdom, let alone, buy it.

There is an erroneous belief abroad in the land of such long standing that most people accept it as truth at some period of their life, and many accept it all their life long. That belief is that in order to acquire or maintain wealth one must of necessity be sinful and dishonest. This error is a two-edged sword, an idea that has cut at the very heart of mankind's welfare for ages. The other sword-edge of this false idea is that, in order to be good or holy or Christian, one must be poor and sad, and generally quite miserable.

Now Jesus was the greatest moralist that ever lived. He held no such views. In fact, He preached quite the opposite. Consider His parable of the Prodigal Son. Is it not a story of a human being trying to live his own life, earn his living as he saw fit, outside his Father's house and rule, only to learn that it is much better to accept all that the Father has to offer? Is it not the story of all of us? Does it not tell us plainly that when we grow tired of poverty and of living with the swine, we can arise (go up higher in our thoughts and understanding of spiritual laws) and go unto our Father who is our God, the Creator, and receive from Him love and riches?

It seems to me that this is the whole purpose of the Prodigal Son parable. You remember that the father in that story did not scold or criticize the wayward son for his mistakes or for using his own judgment. Instead, he ran to meet him, placed a ring on his finger, a symbol of wealth, rejoiced at his return, and gave a welcoming party. The only unhappy person in that story was the brother, who believed that he could somehow be cheated simply because another received. That jealous brother thought it very wrong of his father so to welcome and give to the returning son. The brother represents the average earth-man consciousness. But the father knew that there was plenty for all, including plenty of love and forgiveness and wisdom and the means of sustaining life and making it a pleasant and worthwhile experience.

It is not money which is the root of all evil, but the "love of money." And it certainly is evil, a mistake, to love money for itself alone. We can neither eat it, drink it, nor wear it. It will buy books for us, but not learning. That we must get for ourselves. To love the good things of life is to be grateful for their existence. To love money for itself defeats the purpose for which it was intended. But many people misquote the Bible text and suffer all their lives from poverty because they believe wealth to be sinful.

Another mistake many make about wealth grows out of their peculiar interpretation of the Bible's saying that it is "easier for a camel to go through the eye of a needle than for a rich man to enter the kingdom of heaven."

Jesus was trying to make clear the fact that the kingdom of God is within man; and that it is there we must go for help and ideas. When we are faced with problems we struggle and squirm for the answer and so are forced to think. We even wonder about God in times of great need. But if a man be rich in dollars, if his every physical need has been satisfied through means of gold, he is likely to become so one-sided as to look to material means alone, and never consider morals or spiritual needs. He will not search his own inner self, the very kingdom where God dwells and can always be met.

It is not a sin to be rich. It is a sin to be poor.

Wealth does not mean money or property alone. Wealth includes ideas, morals, spiritual qualities as well as things, goods, and services. This is the kind of wealth or prosperity for which we can pray aright and not amiss. To ask God to prosper you is to ask for an increase in all good.

If your problem has to do with money or wealth you cannot afford to think small, limiting thoughts. If you want to earn an ample income the first thing you must do is to come to a decision about it. For decision is the first step in any journey, the bottom dollar of every fortune, and the first step in getting any desire of your heart.

There are two ways to do things, a long and a short way; a way of working with things on their own plane, using the laws governing them, or of reaching up and getting and using a higher law. That also is arising and going unto the Father.

If you want financial security you can go to school, take specialized training, be educated to a certain profession or business, make yourself valuable to an employer—and so earn. You can work hard, save carefully, deny yourself many comforts and conveniences, allow yourself few or no luxuries, invest carefully and end up in your old age with financial security. There is nothing wrong with that program. By that method many have founded fortunes and found happiness, and have lived useful lives. But it is not the *only* nor the quickest way to found a fortune.

There is a quicker way. You can demonstrate plenty here and now by using prayer and a higher law that supersedes the lower, slower one. This is the method many men who have made great fortunes have used. It is the method that Russell H. Conwell talked so much about in his "Acres of Diamonds" lecture. That whole lecture was based on two truths which he knew, and which are even more workable and important today than they were when he went up and down the country lecturing, because they are more badly needed now than then.

These two truths are: First, to serve or meet a broad human need is a foundation on which to build a fortune. The second truth is that the way to begin is right where one is, without waiting for capital, influence, or any other force outside one's self. Conwell's own life was a proof of the soundness of his preachments.

Conwell gave many instances of people who had created fortunes with new ideas, which they had accepted and *put to work,* ideas that met a human need. (This is waiting on the Lord and being a servant unto Him.) Most of us make the mistake of thinking we must be in competition with others, a notion growing out of a hidden belief in limitation. Over and over Conwell proved he knew the value of prayer and of getting ideas from God.

What Conwell said is so true that anyone can prove it for himself by reflecting a little on the great fortunes made in America. What is the telephone but a servant of human need?—or a railroad, or a steam engine, or a vacuum cleaner, or a windshield wiper, or any and all of the many goods and gadgets that we use so frequently and that once did not exist. Yet the possibility of creating them has always existed. Where were these ideas before some one discovered them? Where was the information about the laws of electricity before Franklin came along with a jar, a kite, and a key? And why is it that relatively only a few discover these fortune-making ideas, when the possibility is open to all?

George A. Hormel, founder of George A. Hormel and Company, once told me that the way to create a fortune is to find a new way to do an old job. Service, he said, was another name for wealth. And is not that true? Is not the telegraph a new way to get a message across the continent? Pony express had been good, but Morse wanted a faster way to deliver messages. It is said that he was spurred on in his investigations and efforts to perfect the telegraph because he had been so deeply touched by the unnecessary deaths of soldiers who had been killed when war had officially ceased, but owing to slowness of messages, the men had fought on. This gives us a hint on how to go about getting fortune-making ideas. And no matter where we look, we shall see this service aspect in fortunes, right down the line, from glass fruit jars to automobiles, to airplanes, and to fountain pens.

If you can discover a human need, and if you honestly want to do something to fulfill that need, then you are already on the way to finding the means to fill it. Your fortune lies in your head and not in some bank. If you do not first draw it out of your head and put it and your-self to work, you will never get it transformed into money in the bank. Ideas are wealth only if put to work. Your ability to think constructive thoughts, to see ways to serve, is your real fortune. What price do you put on your ability to think? Ah, you say, there is not enough money in the world to buy away that priceless treasure. This is silent admission that you realize you can act and nothing can keep you from acting according to what you think.

We are agreed then, are we not, that if you can find a good idea you can make a fortune, if you also put it to work. Where shall you look for that idea?

Within yourself, the only place where you *can* get an idea. Because you must turn within to find God. And this you do through purposeful thinking. Here is the method: First, realize that you live and move and have your be-ing in God, all that is good. Now, get this truth into a picture for better understanding. Imagine God-Mind as the ether around you, covering the city where you live, covering the whole earth, stretching out from our planet in every direction to the farthest ends of the universe. Imagine this ether as a sea in which all the planets, in-cluding our earth, float.

Now, bring the picture closer. Think of this same ether God-Mind as being the same sea in which rests every atom, every electron of all known matter, whether it is the blood, bones, and flesh of your body, the metal of your car, or the petals of a rose. Imagine that the planets and the atoms not only rest or revolve in this Mind-Substance, but that they are held in their respec-tive places by it; that God-Mind fills all space between planets and between atoms alike.

Now we are back where we started from, to that king-dom within yourself. You cannot become aware of this

God-Mind in and through and around you by any of the physical senses. The only way you can get in touch with it is by the means of thought. We live and move and have our being in Him. It is not something away off somewhere, outside ourselves, but "nearer than hands and feet."

Let us look again at this sea of ether. In it dwells all that is, all that was, and all that can be. Every great soul has at some time found it for himself and used it. They tell us about it. Edison went there for all his ideas which became inventions. Marconi, Steinmetz, and our unknown ancestor who invented the wheel; the woman who invented the trolley switch, and one of my friends who invented a new device for spraying cement; all went there for their ideas.

Is this "sea" for inventors only? Oh, no, it is for everyone! Beethoven, Michelangelo, Galileo, Spencer went there for their ideas. Every humble man or woman who prays, "O God, show me what to do!" goes there.

You, too, can go there. You don't need money, capital, or new clothes for the journey. You don't need car or plane fare; you don't need to retire to the country and be alone to invite ideas to come to you that are there in that sea, waiting for anyone who will take hold of them by the means of thought. Stay right where you are. Go into the silence, through your own soul meet God, ask for an assignment of work.

You can tune into God-Mind if you can think. But you must think first! Always, always, you must take the first step. For man has free will. He may choose. Must, for he is not forced. You live and move and have your being, your entire lifetime, in this sea of all there is, or ever shall be. Connect yourself with it. Once you are connected with it, you will find that you alone can break the connection, can stop the stream of ideas, of power, that flow to you. It is something like connecting your electric appliance to the power house. The current is there, instantly, and cannot turn itself off. This is a fact that inventors, composers and writers have proved over and over. Every person of great wealth I have ever known has not only discovered and used this power, but has been happy to acknowledge the fact.

All the creative people I know admit they cannot tell where their best thoughts come from. They only know that they begin thinking in a certain direction because they have *first come to a decision* about some desire, and the needed idea then *comes* to them. This holds true whether it is an idea for creating an entirely new thing, or for handling a customer, or for advertising certain wares, or designing clothes or a house.

The first problem is decision. We must decide what we want, decide that it can be had or done. Then we seek, knock, ask and it is done unto us. The thought we need comes from that sea of all there is. About this Emerson wrote:

"I am constrained every moment to acknowledge a higher origin for events than the will I call mine. As with events, so it is with thoughts . . . I desire and look up and put myself in the attitude of reception, but from some alien energy the visions come."

You may say, "That is very well, if I had leisure and time. But I am chained to my daily job."

This same Russell H. Conwell we have been talking about found time to live two lives! He lived eight hours a day for himself and eight hours a day for little John Ring who had "died for him." Go to your public library and read "Acres of Diamonds." It will give you an idea of how much one man can do.

If you think you have no time to find a new or better work to do, one more to your liking, a fortune to use and share, read how others have done it. Read the autobiography of Benjamin Franklin. He budgeted his time more carefully than most of us ever budget our money. He knew the real value of time. So did Arnold Bennett. Read his *How to Live on Twenty-four Hours a Day.*

When you have done reading you will find you are right where you were—unless in the meantime you have first come to a decision that you can do these same things. Let me repeat: decision is the bottom dollar of every fortune.

It is no use to pray, to receive an idea, if you do not act on it. All of us receive wonderful ideas. We cannot help getting hold of them for the ether is filled with them. The successful people accept them and put them to work. Desire is prayer. Work is prayer. Thinking is prayer. Decision is faith and prayer.

You must see wealth all around you if you are trying to demonstrate wealth. For we are promised "as much as we can see." You must see it in all nature, which is generous in supplying us beyond our own conception. You must rule out all thoughts of limitation. The more you think you can do without the less you will have to do with. The greater the demand on your part, the greater the supply flowing to you from God or nature. Orders are always filled in full.

It is easier and more pleasant to succeed and march forward than it is to stand still, mark time, and think up excuses for your failure. And it certainly is easier to demonstrate prosperity, or constant growth and increase in the good things of life, than it is to exist without them, because to do so is to be in tune with nature. To exist without them is to be out of tune. God gave us our desires so that we would make an effort to fulfill them. Hence, all nature seems to rush to our aid, once we take courage and begin.

Getting the idea is not enough. You must put it to work. Here is an example of what I mean:

A man came to me wanting to know how he and others in his predicament could go about having laws made to force home owners to use architectural plans when building a house. His reasoning was this: Since only about fourteen per cent of all home builders use the services of an architect, and since half the architects are going hungry for lack of work, a law enforcing their services on the public would enable them to earn a living. That was only part of his plan. He would further force the home builder to pay ten per cent of the cost of his home as an architect's fee.

His complaint was that as things stood home owners bought what they thought were plans from banks, material dealers and building companies for as little as twenty dollars. The results, he proved, were shoddy homes, ugly homes, and more expensive homes than would result from high-class plans and protective specifications. His story was one revealing conditions from which everyone suffered because of lack of a better method, lack of information, lack of ideas. He was sure his end justified his means.

In his plan for remedying the situation the architect did not include any idea of how to benefit the home owner or how to serve him any better. He also admitted that such a procedure might prove quite disastrous to home owners, for many architects, he said, knew design better than costs, for example. Such an architect might be permitted to force his plan on a home owner, make him pay the ten per cent and yet find that it would require thousands of dollars more than the owner had expected to spend for a home, in order to produce it from the plans as prepared.

"Well, that happens right along anyhow," the man

said stubbornly. "The home owner would have to know the kind of man to choose, in the first place."

"What about a law to protect home owners?" I said. "From your findings here, it seems just about everyone in the industry is protected but him."

The man was sure the architects needed a law to force their services willy-nilly on the public. But it was a wrong idea and I told him so. It was not an idea of service. It did not benefit the home owner. It offered no way to serve the good contractor who would much rather build by good plans than shoddy ones. His plan would not benefit the material men who might prefer to sell higher-class goods but were prevented from doing so if the plans and specifications did not call for them. No, the man was not thinking of service. He was thinking only of how to earn more money for himself, regardless of others.

The man had overlooked the real point of the whole situation, for there was a grand opportunity for service. I told him to go after a new idea, a plan or method for serving all groups concerned, of bringing them together for the benefit and security of all and not just of himself and his profession. He was to get a plan whereby all would want to co-operate because each would benefit.

The man learned to pray. He got his idea all right, but he let it lie dormant for two years, while he continued to suffer poverty and shame and humiliation through lack of work. Then he came back again for help. I once more urged him to put that good idea to work. But he still wasted time and energy and made excuses to himself for not trying out the plan. After three more years he got started. He earned more in a day than he used to earn in a month, and there seems no limit to his work. Why should there be? Ours is a growing universe. We are a part of that universe, and is not the part like the whole?

Business men say that "the customer gets just what he

pays for." This is true in all life. We get only what we pay for in health, wealth, or happiness. If we want a fortune we must buy it with services to others. If we can serve only one man we get value received. If we can serve a million our pay is in proportion.

If you want the admiration and gratitude of honest men, then you will pay for it by your acts, your character, and your service. But if you would rather have their pity and take a chance on also getting their scorn you will pay for that too; pay for it with dodging and excuses for your failure; with laziness, and lack of either faith or works; pay for it with your envy and hatred of the man who honestly sets out and buys a fortune.

A fortune-making idea need not be a big one. What was the dime store idea but a simple one of better service? A clerk thought it would be a good idea to put a variety of small articles, all the same price, on one table where everyone could see at a glance what he wanted. The idea is still there, earning millions for it was put to work!

All that the Father has is yours. If you do not take it and make use of it to grow and to go forward, you are not living up to your capacity, you are not accepting your own. You are denying Christ. We cannot make full use of what we have here on earth, for it is here in such profusion and plenty, and what we do not yet see is also waiting for us. There is so much available that civilized countries are now destroying such necessities as food and plowing under cotton, in order to keep up prices. What idea is needed here? Is this the problem *you* are to solve?

Do you really want wealth? Do you want to be prospered beyond your present dreams? Then try this: Go into your closet—I mean a closet or a very small room. Close the door. See that it is dark. Get down on your knees. Close your eyes and become as physically still as you possibly can. You need not say a word, at first. Just be quiet, and be conscious of the fact that you are there for only one purpose: to meet God. If you have a childish picture of God as a man with a white beard sitting on a golden throne, then do not use the term God. Say "Great Infinite Spirit."

Do not be discouraged if it takes a good many times for you to get any seeming response out of this willingness on your part to commune with God. Be patient. Keep right on trying.

Sooner or later you will become aware that some kind of contact is actually being made. If you cannot speak your desire, then be content for awhile to think it. By practice you will be able to make an instant contact. Then say, whispering, "Great Infinite Spirit, I thank thee for my wealth of life, love, wisdom, and growth."

What good is it to pray for a thousand or ten thousand dollars, if you have not the wisdom or the love to use it instead of letting it abuse you? What good to ask for a certain job because you think it will bring the money you need, if you have not the wisdom to know whether it would be keeping you from an even better and more satisfying one? What good indeed, to ask for and receive wealth, if you have not the wisdom to keep it from robbing you of further growth? For growth is the purpose of all life. To give that up is to lose your own soul. In the final analysis, we want wealth because we want the things it will buy, because we believe such things will enable us to live better, to have more of life.

But, someone may object, how can I honestly thank God for what I do not have? If I had it I would not need to be asking.

Jesus had his prayers answered. He said that we must ask in effect as though we had already received. I do not know why the great Infinite Spirit moves in our behalf when we use the law in this manner, or rather, when we work inside that law, asking, giving thanks that we have already received. But I do know it is so. I am sure there is nothing mysterious about it, any more than there is about the process of magnetizing a piece of steel.

In truth you *do* have a wealth of life, love, wisdom, and growth. More than you will ever use! Your prayer is your witness to God and to yourself that you are tired of eating husks, tired of the company of poverty and that you are now ready to arise and go unto your Father, where you in your secret heart always have known, but for a while neglected to remember, that there is a welcome and all that the Father hath, waiting for you.

Try it, my friend! I promise you that if you will be faithful in your prayer, God will prosper you. Ideas will come. New opportunities will open. Facts will become significant. In short, you will see the Father running to meet you, coming to welcome you, to pour out His love and His good upon you.

CHAPTER EIGHT

Praying for Health

CAN HEALTH BE RESTORED through prayer? Is there such a thing as a faith healing? I say yes. I say that physical, mental, and spiritual health can be restored and maintained by means of prayer. Not by the fear-inspired, distorted mumble-jumble that many people believe to be prayer. Words of fear indicate a hope that is dead. Such prayers are more than likely to drive trouble deeper. Life alone can impart life. The prayer that heals is the prayer of Truth, Life, and Love. Jesus used the prayer of absolute faith and knowingness. He did not faintly hope his prayers would heal. He *knew* they would.

If any man will dig deeply enough into his own consciousness he will know that prayer can heal. This is wisdom native to all, which through the ages of civilization has been covered over with doubts, fears, customs, and creeds, and in the last two thousand years with ecclesiasticism and dogma. Preaching the gospel alone has come down to the church. Through the years the healing part of religion has been largely dropped or left to other agencies than the church.

Jesus was known as the Great Physician. He used prayer to restore health. Of His thirty-three recorded miracles, we find that twenty-four had to do with healing, restoring health. If we study the life and works of Jesus we see that He was not content to minister to the Spirit only, but healed the body and mind as well. Further, Jesus instructed His Disciples to go about healing as well as teaching.

We are coming back to the idea of healing the sick and preaching the gospel as belonging together and being inseparable, as they were in the days of Jesus. We are coming to it through the findings of modern science. Psychology, psychiatry, and psychosomatic treatment are being accepted today as never before. And with good reason. Man is three in one. If a sick mind or a sick spirit dwell in a body, it will sicken the body at least to some degree. Medical men today are taking thought histories as well as physical histories of their patients.

I have nothing to say against the medical profession. Personally, I think that a good doctor must of necessity also be a good person, a good soul. Nurses are certainly angels in disguise. Hospitals are institutions of mercy. I do not think that the human race could have progressed as rapidly as it has without the aid of the medical profession and all that it means.

The danger lies in our accepting medicine and surgery as the highest and final method of healing. If we compare the need of healing with the need of light we get a larger view of the truths involved. If a man's house is not wired for electricity, he shows good sense to use a kerosene lamp or a candle, or even a burning pine knot, rather than to sit in the dark. If a man is ill he had better call in a doctor and thank God for him, if he does not know a higher law of healing and how to use it. But to say that such a law does not exist is to believe in a limited universe, as well as to deny Christ.

Can it be that America, said to be the richest country in the world, is also the most ailing in health? We are told by our lawyers that one in every thirty-seven is a criminal, and by our doctors that there are more patients in mental institutions than the total number of patients for all other diseases combined, including our well-known killers: heart disease, cancer, and tuberculosis. There are more cases of *dementia præcox* than of tuberculosis alone, to say nothing of the other mental diseases. What is wrong with our way of life that such terrifying figures are true?

Dr. Kenneth E. Appel, Assistant Professor of Psychiatry of the University of Pennsylvania Medical School, stated that he believed this appalling situation was owing largely to the way parents and schools bring up our youth. He considers our methods "too soft, indulgent, and unrealistic."

Another doctor, a psychiatrist, who has served on an Army-Navy induction center examining board for several years and whose duty it was to determine whether the inductee was mentally fit to enter the armed services, gives me this enlightening information:

He says his questioning of the inductees has revealed the fact that almost eighty per cent of them have had little or no religious training, have little or no religious convictions, yet all "believe in a Supreme Power of some kind." Which is tantamount to saying that while these young men are aware that God exists (it is my own personal opinion that no one ever loses his consciousness of God) that they *never learned how to communicate with Him.* There is the trouble, it seems to me. They never learned how to pray, perhaps never had tried, or, having tried wrongly and having failed, they gave up trying.

Can any one logically deny that prayer has a disciplining effect on the minds and characters, the morals of all who earnestly try it?

Oh, yes, someone may agree, we could doubtless decrease our crime rate and our mental illness rate by seeing that every child received a good religious training. But— But it is hopeless to try to heal your own mind and spirit and body by the means of prayer, by the means of faith, religion applied?

That is the trouble. We fear it will not work, for us. For the other fellow, maybe, but not for us? Let's talk about you and your health problem.

Health is the normal condition. Ill health results from a lack or a superfluity. Perfect health is a perfect balance of needs being met (intake) and of discards being eliminated or energy consumed. There is no reason why a man cannot grow old as gracefully, as beautifully, and with no more illness than is experienced by a perfect oak tree. Ill health or dying young serves no known need of God or man.

There are two ways to restore health: a long way and a short way. The long way round is to go to a competent and honest physician and have proper tests and examinations made. He will first seek the cause. In looking for the cause he will look into the body, mind, and spirit. He will consider diet, all kinds of personal habits. If still puzzled he may call in a surgeon, a psychologist, or a psychiatrist. For he knows the real cause may be hidden in any one of the three component parts of the patient. And I lately heard an excellent physician lecture on the fact that it also "takes religion to heal a man."

Doctors tell us that hospitals house many people who are there only because they are happier being sick than they are being well and assuming their responsibilities, a fact that they have not recognized, probably, and could not entertain without shock. They are sick in spirit. Prayer will certainly heal the spirit.

What is the matter with these people who take to their bed to be loved and cared for while they pretend to be children? The doctors say they have perhaps met with some problem which they could not solve and so they retreated to the safety of illness. The truth is that such people have broken contact with God; have lost sight of their real identities, their perfect selves. They have lost

sight of the source of real love, of health and security.
Some such people with whom I have worked have recovered when they found they did not have to depend upon
any one certain person, place, or thing to solve the problems of their lives. When they found God consciously,
they were able to build new hopes and so new lives. They
had lost the old childhood conception of God and had
not, as adults, found "a God to take His place." Their
lives and spirits had become frustrated, their views distorted. Prayer certainly heals such sickness as that.

Again, doctors find much mental illness that is but an
illusion behind which the patient hides. Back of that is
perhaps a deeply buried emotion of hatred, desire for
revenge, or deep-seated fear. It may be a fear of not
enough money to meet bills, or a fear of no life after
death. Such sufferers are often found to believe in a law
of limitation. Their whole lives are bound up in fears.

Illness may result from a hidden sense of shame or of
being rejected as less than, or unworthy of, certain persons or all persons. This could not happen if the patient
kept his contact with God. I once worked with a woman
who had several times attempted suicide. She had been
hospitalized and given many treatments, including that of
"learning to use her hands in order to heal her mind," as
she put it. But once out of the hospital the old frenzy
returned. She was suffering from a burden of a sense of
guilt that was too heavy to bear. She was healed only
after she was convinced by her own inner consciousness
that "God did not wish to punish her, and was not doing
so; that the punishment came from her own thinking."

Much illness in the body has been found to be objectified worry or hate or fear of one kind or another. It has
been found that such things as stomach ulcer may be nothing more than objectified worry. What shall we do in
such a case? Cut the ulcer out and let the patient worry

about the bills, and so acquire a new ulcer? Or shall we show the patient how to pray, how to stop worry and fret, and to convince him that he is immortal and help him to a new outlook on life? To get a true conception of God and man's relation to Him is to do away forever with petty worries and cares, hates and fears. That is the short way of making one whole—by prayer.

People talk themselves into more trouble and actual illness than they may realize. Proverbs is filled with excellent advice on how to keep well. Consider the following: "The mouth of a righteous man is a well of life." What beautiful poetry and what absolute truth! Also: "Can a man take fire in his bosom, and his clothes not be burned?" Can a man take ill will, hatreds, fears, doubts, and worries into his bosom, his heart, his consciousness, without his physical body showing the result?

We have been told that every word we speak will have to be, and is, accounted for. For every word we utter produces after its kind. Oh, to learn to speak words of life and love and wisdom, and never to waste breath on words of illness, limitation, bitterness! "He that keepeth his mouth keepeth his life."

That one's thoughts and ideas of life have an effect upon the physical body has long been known. "Any nobleness begins at once to refine a man's features; any meanness or sensuality to imbrute," said Thoreau. So it does, but not only the features. The very organs of the body, the blood stream, the thoughts, the attitude toward life and God all are affected by our nobleness or our meanness. And over that we have control.

Ralph Waldo Emerson was a great soul; he was one of the wisest Americans who ever lived. Emerson had a wonderful spiritual insight. On one occasion he writes, "O my brothers, God exists!" And in his essay on the intellect he says:

"Every substance is negatively electric to that which stands above it in the chemical tables, positively to that which stands below. Water dissolves wood and iron and salt; air dissolves water; electric fire dissolves air, but the intellect dissolves fire, gravity, laws, method, and the subtlest unnamed relations of nature in its resistless menstruum."

What Emerson says shows us both the long and the short way to restore health. We can find on their own plane the means and methods of dissolving the trouble, of learning how to kill disease germs for example, by learning "what stands above" them. There is nothing wrong with working on this plane in which the disease or ill health seems to appear. But neither is there anything wrong in reaching up for a higher law and using it. The intellect does indeed dissolve any obstruction that has been built up by fear or false ideas. This intellect is prayer. Jesus used prayer to dissolve unwholesome conditions in the body, even to cleansing the lepers of that day. He drove out "devils" from the mind and spirit. The late Dr. Alexis Carrel, author of *Man, the Unknown,* tells of seeing a cancer heal, shrivel, dry up, at Lourdes, where so many miracles have been wrought.

When treating for health in this shorter way, by prayer, you need not understand what is wrong as a physician or surgeon understands it. You need not know "the subtlest unnamed relations of nature" nor why a cancer builds itself out of good blood and healthy cells into a horrible growth that consumes the host on which it feeds. You need know nothing of cell growth in order to be rid of ulcer, cancer, tumor, or any other growth or condition. You need only know how to commune with God, and to wait on the Lord and never once doubt while you are waiting.

We have kept repeating these steps in prayer of asking

aright, in faith believing and in waiting on the Lord. We can afford to. Is not that just what Jesus did when He healed? Let us look at His works and see if we can discover some underlying method.

We find that in healing Jesus used the words, "Thy sins are forgiven." He rebuked His disciples for failing to heal, for not having enough faith. He frequently gave thanks during healings, and at the time of raising Lazarus from the dead He gave thanks before he even tried to make this greatest of healings.

Again Jesus seemed always to get the consent of his patient before He tried to heal him. Perhaps it means that no man can be healed against his will; that free will gives us the right to suffer if we want to; the right to hold back our own soul growth, if we prefer to shirk life's problems, and so, become ill subconsciously in order to avoid them. Jesus seemed at least to satisfy Himself of the patient's genuine desire to be healed. It would seem that the patient's honest, sincere desire to be healed was equivalent to his "saying the word," and also in asking aright.

The above would cover our first two steps in our method of demonstration. As to the third, that of waiting on the Lord, being willing to be a servant unto God, we know that Jesus' teaching over and over covered that point. For example:

Jesus taught the importance of brotherly love, of our forgiving one another in our every day life, for wholeness of living. You remember the facts as recorded in Matthew, where the lawyer asked Jesus what was the most important commandment and Jesus replied: "Thou shalt love the Lord thy God with all thy heart, and with all thy soul, and with all thy mind. This is the first and great commandment. And a second is like unto it, Thou

shalt love thy neighbor as thyself. On these two commandments hang all the law and the prophets."

Is not that a plain command to become a servant of the
Lord if we want all good reflected in our life? The point
many of us so often overlook is that we are to love ourselves and our neighbor. Too often we think this means
to love our neighbor more and ourselves less. I think it
means that we are to think well of ourselves. I have
never met a person (I do not say they do not exist) who
thought as well of himself as he might.

I have helped people with a very simple prayer, a statement of facts as I see them. Your way of healing may be
much better. But this is a way I have found good: Seeing
that we have free will and that in exercising it we are
quite likely to make a mistake (commit a sin), and seeing that this can happen even when we are not aware
that it is taking place or has taken place, it follows that
before healing can be manifest the mistake must be
righted, the sin forgiven. Even with our own careless
words we condemn ourselves and sin against our bodies.

Therefore I instruct the sick person to pray in this
wise: "God forgive me and make me whole." It is simple, direct, yet it covers all the points of prayer. There
is no attempt to understand what is wrong, no attempt to
right it. It is all left up to God. The prayer is a confes-
sion that something has gone wrong, that not God but the
person has made a mistake. It is an admission that God
will hear and right the mistake. By repeating the prayer
the patient opens up his whole being to the inflow of God
ideas. Spirit is left free to work, and the demonstration
is made. Often the patient becomes acutely aware of
some mistake he has been making. He realizes he cannot long continue in it and also continue to ask God's
help, if he is sincere in his desire to be healed. And he

has learned that an attempt to do so is to divide his house —work against himself.

A bedridden woman used this prayer, realizing she had an excellent opportunity to devote her waking hours to prayers for health. She began by the method I advise, giving thanks, blessing all with whom one comes in contact and expecting a change for the better. She began thanking God for the help of all who served her, for their strong bodies, their training, and their kindness. "It would take hours," she said, "to bless by name all those responsible for a good breakfast in bed." Her oft-repeated and sincerely felt "Thank you, God," had its effect. One day it came to her that something she had been thinking about her sister-in-law was wrong. She had long been telling it as true. She eventually felt "her mistake had been wiped out and forgiven by God." She further felt she wanted to know God's will and to follow it, always. She was healed.

Another woman was healed by simply thinking this prayer. She tried to say the words, but no words would come. Each morning at ten she went into her clothes closet, closed the door and stood in the dark. She wanted to be made well. She wanted to correct any mistake she had made that might have caused suffering to others or herself. She wanted to "live anew." She would put her arms against the wall and lean her head on them and just stand there, silent.

One day the thought came to her that just standing there was all she had to do. It was in effect acknowledging the fact that God heard and would answer. By her very desire to find God and her faith that she would find Him, she was actually praying. After that it did not bother her that no words came. It did not bother her that the healing did not come. She was willing to "wait on the Lord" in time, and in her daily life she became a servant unto Him, discovering many ways to show kindness and gratitude and to serve others. She read widely such books and articles as would help her increase her faith in the goodness of God, nature, and the universe.

Finally, the time came when it seemed that something was being said to her, mentally. After that she went into the closet for the definite purpose of listening. To the extent that she could screen out all her problems and thoughts about herself and just remember she was there to meet God, to that extent "something told her things."

One day, when in that listening attitude, the thought came to her that her body did not matter, sick or well. She was told quite plainly that the soul was all, that it was indestructible and could never be made sick or hurt. She felt a wonderful lightness, a lifting up throughout her whole being. She felt she "need never worry again about anything that concerned her physical body." From that day her happiness increased. Her worry went away and the healing took place when she had, she said, "forgotten all about it."

In this case the woman never did know what she had done or thought or said that was wrong and that had reflected as illness. She did not need to know. Neither do you need to know what caused your illness in order to be able to heal it.

Other healings have taken place as a result of reading uplifting literature. The patient has been completely taken out of himself, has been convinced that prayer is answered, and in that deep and perfect conviction has tried it and been healed.

Healings have taken place from listening to uplifting music. Just how this happens I do not know. Since every atom of our physical being is subject to laws of vibration and movement, it may be they respond in some way. We know that Caruso could break a glass by singing to it. It may be that on hearing the music for some time the patient puts himself in tune with the lofty thought of the composer. Thus he lifts himself out of the consciousness of his pain-torn body and sees nothing but perfection, nothing but his real spiritual self and so, the instant he lets go, is healed.

If you are ill it can do no harm to try music and prayer together. Many people use inspiring music to wash away the cares of the day and to create the mood of worship before they go into the silence to pray. And why not? The great musicians, the great composers, got their harmonies from God. Musicians listen to something inside themselves and copy down as faithfully as possible what they hear, and we call them composers. They have tuned in to the divine source of all there is. You can do the same and induce spiritual power to flow through you, healing each cell, making your health perfect.

Certain it is that no sincere prayer leaves us where it finds us. Every thought we entertain about drawing near to God strengthens us just that much and makes us that much more able to understand all life and to face all the problems that come. For problems are but opportunities to grow. It never is what happens that hurts, but what we think about it. Prayer keeps reminding us that the new situation which we face is not a stumbling-block but a stepping-stone that leads upward.

From the beginning of time, it seems, people have struggled with health problems. That is an unavoidable result of our having free will. It is just as easy for us to create an evil in our lives as it is for us to create a good. Even David did not escape health problems. He says in the twenty-seventh *Psalm*, "I had fainted, unless I had believed to see the goodness of the Lord in the land of the living." Again in the fifty-sixth *Psalm* he says, "For thou hast delivered my soul from death: wilt not thou deliver my feet from falling, that I may walk before God in the light of the living?"

If, like the man we talked about in previous chapters, we would start the practice of praying without ceasing, we would get and maintain perfect health. It could not be otherwise. Our trouble is that during the times when things seem to be going right we forget God. Then we think and act accordingly. One day we are quite conscious of something being wrong. We call it sickness. It is an accumulation of sick thoughts, fear thoughts, anger thoughts, and other negative thoughts which have drawn their physical counterpart to us. Our words "have been made flesh" and dwell with us. We forget our Divine source. We fret and hurry and worry. We over eat and under exercise. Or we under eat and over worry. We tie our nerves into knots. We have taken upon ourselves all the burdens of life, forgetting they rightly belong to God who created us and put us here on earth for some purpose of His own and so is responsible for us.

Health is a personal and civic duty. I believe the time will come when society will look upon the habitual poverty-stricken person and the habitual sick person as it looks upon the habitual criminal today. We are learning so much about spiritual laws and how to work in accord with them in living a full life and in being self-helpful that there will be little excuse, if any, to fail and to ask society to carry us along. Such failures will be no less law-breakers than is the criminal of today.

We shall have more physicians learning Jesus' method of healing. Doctors of the future will not so often say, "Put the patient in the hospital and operate." They will say, "Put the patient in the hospital and learn what's wrong with his thinking." And when they find out, they can say "Take up thy bed and walk." For there will be great hospitals wherein people are taught how to think their way to health by learning spiritual laws and keeping them. That day is coming for all men and every good metaphysician who has seen faith or prayer healings taking place knows it is coming. And more doctors are trying to bring that day closer than some may realize.

Are you ill? Then search your secret heart for hidden and perhaps previously unnoticed or unacknowledged negative thoughts and feelings. What do you fear? Whom do you hate? What is the most annoying thing in your daily life? Are you leaving a duty undischarged that silently tugs at your conscience for attention? Does your inner life or soul approve of your thoughts and acts? Have you a hope long deferred, or a dream you'd like to bring into reality, but fear it can never come to life? Do you believe civilization is going backward and that life is all in vain?

Remember, *every* thought you entertain reflects in your physical body, your conscious mind, and your affairs. In the name of God and perfect health, give up every sour, unhappy, impatient, and intolerant thought. Give up and cast out every fear and regret and every feeling of shame. You are a child of God!

Begin today to seek God. Go into your closet. Still all outside claims and interferences. Say "God forgive me and make me whole." Have faith and persistence and wait on the Lord and you will be made whole!

CHAPTER NINE

Praying for Power

WE ARE TRYING to change our lives from what they are to what we want them to be. We are tired of poverty, tired of failure, tired of our old humdrum jobs. We want to leave our feeling of frustration of the present and anxiety of the future behind us. We want to produce more, be more. We want to have more security and more freedom than we ever have known. We want more love, beauty and peace in our lives. We want what Jesus was talking about—to have life and to have it more abundantly!

Oh, if we but had the power to soar out and up and away from this drab existence. If we could but wake up tomorrow in a bright new world. If we but had the power? Power? What *is* power?

According to Webster, power is "the ability, whether physical, mental, or moral, to act; the faculty of doing or performing something; capacity for action or performance or for receiving external action or force."

That gives us something to work on. What we really want then, is the *ability to act* and the *ability to receive external action* or *force,* which implies action or force in our belief.

Let us start our search for power by first looking into the possibility of receiving external force which will help us solve our problems.

A little clear thinking brings us to the conclusion that all human beings, whether the head hunter in the jungle or a fortune hunter in Wall street, realize there is an external force or power to which they can appeal for help. Their different methods of approach to this power and their different beliefs about what it is and how to use it vary with the level of intelligence or learning of the individuals using it. The significant thing is that they *all believe.* They do not all try to call on the power. But they all know it exists. And when one does call on that power for help, he gets it according to his understanding of the power and the amount or weight of his belief in it.

It is my personal conviction that every living thing is aware of this power. I believe all units of life use it and in most instances obey its dictates without question and, in some instances, without the possibility of choice. I think in no other way can we, for example, explain the perfect formation in flight of certain shore birds, the migration of birds and animals, and the almost human intelligence many of them display. I further believe that it is through this power that we are able to meet with the intelligence of the lower animals in working with them. I am sure that in varying degrees this same power lies in every atom in the universe, whether that atom be of gold, flesh, flower, or star.

I further believe that the healing agency in medicine, vitamins, minerals, and the building blocks in calories resides in this power inherent in them.

If the birds of the field, the plants of the earth, the stars in their courses, and the waters in their falling know and use this power, can not you and I also use it? Does not man have dominion over all?

Jesus of Nazareth was a man who knew and used this power which has ever since been termed Christ power. Where did He get this power? What was it? How did He get the "capacity for action and performance" which we have since termed the miracles? On what did His capacity for "receiving external action or force" consist and what external action or force came to Him? And why?

We know that Jesus' use of this power proved beyond all doubt that man can control his circumstances instead of being controlled by them. That is what we want to do, is it not? Jesus said that of Himself He could do nothing; that He, the mortal man, the citizen of Nazareth could do nothing and that the Father in him did the works. Well then, what *is* the Father? Our Creator, God.

Now we have the secret of it all. The power we want is already ours. It is our share or portion of *God-Mind*. We have a share of ultimate truth, beauty, wisdom, life —all that God is. It is our ability to create, to hope, to love, to worship, to learn, and to live forever. But how large a portion is our share?

Jesus said there was no limit except that which we ourselves place upon it. We have as much as we believe in and will call on and use. The power is not outside us, not in the mountain, not in Jerusalem, no, but exactly where Jesus said it was—within us. Here is the foundation of the New Thought religion. We do not have to ask or beg for this power! It is already ours, here and now, awaiting our word or direction. It lies there, inactive, until we release it by our words.

"All that the Father hath" is ours, yours and mine. That is a fact which should send us to our knees in awe and jubilation, did we but understand the smallest part of it. Jesus knew and promised that we could do even greater than He did. I have not the slightest doubt that we shall learn and do even more than He did. But long before we have learned even a fraction as much as He knew, we can have learned enough to change our lives

from what they are to what we want them to be. And
the way to learn is by prayer.

In a previous chapter we discussed *God-Mind* as a sea
of ether in and around and through us, permeating every
cell of our bodies and brains, every particle of space in
the universe. We said that it is to this sea-of-all-there-is
that we can go for ideas. We can go there for power,
actual mountain-moving power, according to Jesus Christ
and according to modern science.

Modern science says space is charged with energies
(which means power) that would transform the earth—
if we knew how and could control them. Sir Oliver Lodge
said that a single cubic inch of ether contains energy
enough to run a forty-horse-power engine forty million
years! Jesus said that if we had faith as of a grain of
mustard seed we could move mountains. Only one energy
in the universe; one energy of many forms.

And how shall we induce this power or energy to move
in our behalf? By thinking. On the physical plane we
can burn coal and release the energy in it. On the mental
plane we can use thought to release and direct this one
energy of the universe. On the spiritual plane we can
release this energy through love and faith.

It comes down to this then: we do not have to create a
power. All the power there is or ever shall be already
exists. We need only learn how to release it, how to
direct it to do our bidding. Man has free will. He, like
God, can and does create. Nor can he help creating. His
every word creates after its kind. His every thought
creates. Words and thoughts are commands for this
power to act. And it does act, whether our word be a
curse or a blessing, our desire be to destroy or to create.

What we need to learn is how to use this power wisely.
We have already learned that unless we use it for good
for all, that we will not have solved our problem but

have created a new and worse one. We want to live, therefore, we desire bread. But if we murder in order to get money to buy bread we have not solved our problem but have created a new one. We have to learn to lean not on our own understanding, but to consult God in everything.

What do *you* want? Use the power that Christ used, pay for it and take it! What will it cost you? It will cost you *decision, knowledge, faith,* and *works.* These will release and direct the power that waits to serve you.

You must decide. This is in effect placing your order for what you want. It notifies nature that here is one who intends to accomplish. You alone must decide what you want, decide you can get it, decide where and when and how to start, and decide that you will then keep on and on. God Himself cannot give you your heart's desire until you know definitely what it is you do want. Decision releases power and directs it.

Having vague thoughts and wishes about what you want to do with life will give you no happiness and no success whatever. Few people ever know what they really want of life. But those who do know exactly what they want, and want it badly enough, always get it. Because decision has the power to open the way to opportunity. It draws strong people who help and breeds success in whatever it touches.

After coming to your decision you must take the next step: you must gather knowledge about your desire so that you will know how to go about achieving it and how further to direct the power that is already within you. This is active prayer. Applied knowledge is power. It does no good to possess the knowledge unless it is used.

The world of affairs is organized for people who know what they want. The world stands ready to help the person who sets out to help himself or to bring about

needed reforms that help all men. For all men know
what is good and right and Christ-like. Many people
think they must have money or influence before they can
begin a project of mercy or reform. They ascribe too
much power to money. If money had as much power as
we commonly give it, why do we see rich men's sons lack
even the power to hold on to the fortunes they inherit?
If money meant power, then only the wealthy would ever
have power, and no poor boy would ever be able to start
from the bottom and create a fortune. The truth is the
other way around; he who uses the power he has can
create a fortune or anything else that he wants.

A thousand hands stretch out to help the one who
starts out to help himself and others, for such a one has
given notice to the world that he is aware of his power
and that he intends to use it. The world loves people who
do things and honors those who do them well. And the
top performers are handsomely paid. Why not? Our
hero and fan worship grow out of a very fine instinct. We
are saying that we not only approve and laud, but we do
so because we know that we too could do better than we
do; and we enjoy living vicariously in the life of the hero
whom we worship. We admire those who have used their
power better than we have used ours. We are grateful to
them for silently reminding us of our own inheritance.

Having come to your decision, gathered information
and knowledge about the thing you want to do, you now
have to invest your faith in your project.

Some of my students achieve a state of constant faith
by what I term the lump-sum method. They accept God
as their Creator, themselves as immortal, and the world
as a training school in which they cannot fail. They go
about their business of asking and getting answers as
naturally as they eat or sleep. Ways open to them as if
by magic. They make friends who go out of their way to

help. Talents and abilities blossom forth that they once did not suspect they possessed. They lead a charmed life.

Others find it hard to develop a working faith. If you belong to this type, take it in easy steps and make each one sure, and try little things first so that you may gain faith in accomplishment. Accomplish them; then try others. Every thought of faith is added to the total store.

I know a woman who is developing her faith by the step-method. For a long time she practised on "setting her mind," so that she would wake up at an exact time every morning. After she became perfect at that she started other tasks. Always she thought in terms of God's doing the work, of turning within to the power that is in direct contact with God-Mind everywhere. This is what Jesus meant when he said that none could go to the Father except through Him (Christ). He did not mean the mortal man Jesus of Nazareth, but the inner soul or mind which He said we all have.

One day this woman couldn't find a pair of scissors that she needed badly. Before her campaign to develop constant faith she would have spent time and energy looking blindly for them. Now she sat down and quietly realized that there is but one Mind; that her individual mind was connected with it, being a part of it; that anything in God-Mind could be reached by her individual mind, and that the solution to any problem she ever could or would have would be found in God-Mind.

After awhile the woman thought to look in the bottom drawer of the linen chest, between the last two sheets. There she found the scissors, where her daughter doubtless had misplaced them in putting away the clean laundry, after using them to cut the string around the bundle. The woman never would have thought of looking there by the old trial-and-error method.

The problem was little, but the principle was the same

one that moves mountains—the same one that carries
you from where you are to where you want to go—to success, service, and happiness. By making that little demonstration the woman was just that much nearer the bigger
ones she was some day going to make, just as the athlete
is nearer perfection every time he goes through the paces
successfully.

You have come to a decision, gathered knowledge, and
generated faith. There then remains the last step: work.
That will take time and energy. But you have plenty of
both and to spare. It takes time and energy to fail, as
Dorothea Brande points out in her book *Wake Up and
Live.*

How then shall you set to work to achieve your big
purpose in life? By doing the first thing first, then the
second, leaving nothing out until the end is done. This is
prayer without ceasing. Said Josiah Gilbert Holland:

> "Heaven is not reached at a single bound;
> But we build the ladder by which we rise
> From the lowly earth to the vaulted skies,
> And we mount to its summit round by round."

Step by step, round by round! It is just as easy for you
to become the highest paid and best man in your chosen
work as it is to remain at the bottom round. As easy?
Easier!

It is easier to succeed greatly than it is to fail miserably.
Why? Because once you get off that bottom round, you
find less competition, fewer hopeless thoughts around you,
a less discouraging atmosphere, less obstruction in your
way. Every round you go up thereafter means thinner
crowds and fewer irritations. The higher you go the
freer you are to accomplish your goal. Also, you will find
more intelligent people who not only understand what you
are trying to do but will help you do it. You will find,

up there, people who make good instead of making excuses. They are the ones who have discovered that all constructive work, done in a right attitude, is prayer.

There always is more room at the top than there is at any other place on the ladder of success. That is because most people have so little faith in themselves, change their decisions so often, and attempt to accomplish their work with such feeble efforts that they remain on the bottom.

What do you want? Fame? You have all the power there is in the universe at your disposal just as you have all the oxygen there is for your breathing. If you set out merely to win fame and fortune, regardless, you probably never will get there. That is not the recipe. A great voice teacher tells me that when a student comes to him saying, "How soon can I get a radio contract?" or, "How soon can I get into the opera?" he does not take that student. He says he never has known even a very talented singer to win success that way. He says the talented ones win success by wanting to sing so greatly that they take the necessary pains to learn the right way. They develop the power that is in them. When they finally do learn, he says, their joy in expressing themselves is so immense, their own thrill so tremendous, that they automatically thrill others. The public demands to hear them sing. Fame and fortune have been achieved as a result, not as a goal. To sing beautifully and perfectly was the goal. To ask to be able to do so was asking aright.

This holds true in every walk of life. The one who works for money never earns as much as the one who loves his work so intensely that if he didn't have to earn a living he would go on doing it for pleasure. That is praying while you work and making your work a prayer.

But if you do want fame there is one infallible recipe

and you already have the power to achieve it. You have but to release that power. The one thing that never fails to lift a human being out of the ordinary class and place him in the honored-of-men class is service to mankind.

Lincoln was an ordinary man who loved people. He wanted to serve people. What he knew of psychology, statesmanship and economics came from the Bible. What he knew of the needs of the people came from his heart. He was a man who knew God, who knew how to pray.

People come to me saying, "Yes, I know my life has been a kind of failure. I haven't done much but just live. Used to think I'd like to do something for humanity, but I'm too old now. Not enough time left." To all such I say:

"An average lifetime is 70 years. That means 840 months, or 3640 weeks, or 25,568 days, or 613,632 hours. But that is not all. Every hour has 60 minutes, so in 70 years you have 36,817,920 minutes which is 2,209,-075,200 seconds. And it takes only *one* second to get a flash, a new insight into life and living, possibilities that will change your whole life, and perhaps the whole mode of living for the world, eventually. The trouble is not with time. You have plenty of that. Your trouble is that you do not purpose in your heart. You have not come to a decision. Because if you had, that would be asking for it; and if you really wanted to do something, that would be asking aright. And if you asked and truly wanted to do something, you would have faith and would be willing to wait on the Lord. Nothing keeps you from success but yourself."

Such people have thought they could kill time, only to find that wasted time kills them, kills faith, ambition, and ability. But one earnest desire can start it all to life again. Always, always, the Father runs to meet us when

we become disgusted with our miserable failures and arise
and start to Him.

There are other people who come to me saying, "I
want to do thus and so, but I am afraid I can't because
of my inherited traits and my past or present environment." Then they tell me a long story about how their
childhood was ruined and their education neglected and,
therefore, that even though they have a desire to do a
thing, it would be useless for them to attempt it. In other
words, they believe they have a desire but not the power
to fulfill it. To such I say:

"Your inheritance goes back through all your ances-
tors to Adam, to God. Draw out the good from all of
them and discard anything you don't want. Environment
means the thoughts you live in and not the house and
neighborhood. It means your hopes, your whole attitude
toward life, God, and the universe, and not what your
neighbors do or fear or think of you."

I tell them that "Inheritance can give you red hair and
a straight nose. Environment can give you habits of saying 'You all,' or of eating with your knife. These two
function on the physical and the mental planes, respectively. They are the two lower planes. There is a higher
one which overcomes the lower ones. There is a power,
when appealed to, which can overcome every handicap of
inheritance and environment to the end that you can live
a happy, useful life and can accomplish wonders."

"That power is what I call God's Guarantee to the
individual. Through no fault of his own, the individual
is given certain parents, and is placed, at least for awhile,
in certain environments—two factors in his life beyond
his control. It may be said that such a one is born with
two strikes against him. But God is fair. His guarantee
to the individual reads like this: If you have a *desire* to
do a thing, count it as proof positive that you can do it.

Desire and fulfillment are two sides to one whole. If it were not possible for you to fulfill the desire, it would not be possible to entertain it either. The desire is God's silent plea to let Him work through you. It is God's silent guarantee that He will see you through if you will but begin."

Yes, my friends, each of us has a work to do. We are not forced to do it. The more sorely we are dissatisfied with our situation in life, the more tormented we are by an urge to do a thing, the more sure it is that God is inviting us to take the step. Always, always, the urge is the silent invitation on the one hand, and the guarantee of our success, if we will make the attempt, on the other.

What do *you* want? It is yours for the taking. Ah, my friend, you are immortal! God exists. You have the same power within you that Christ had within Him. Believe it, use it, and you cannot hope too much, nor dare too much. For in Him you live and move—forward, forevermore!

CHAPTER TEN

Praying for Love

As WE HAVE BEEN discussing the possibility of changing
our lives through prayer there has been a silent question
in our minds which must now be considered openly. We
have been asking: *Can we change the world through
prayer?*

For as this is written World War Two is raging. We
ask ourselves and each other, "Will it happen again?"
Already there are threats of the third World War. Our
lives and liberties have become so bound up in the problems growing out of this and the last World War that
there is turmoil, grief, and sadness on every hand. We
have a right to here ask whether we can change the world
through prayer.

Einstein said that if two per cent of the people of the
world decided there *should* be no more war there *could*
be no more war! I agree. For history shows us con-
clusively that the world's affairs and policies always have
been dictated and run by a few strong leaders. The rest
of us follow like sheep, or worse, allow ourselves to be
herded like cattle.

Can we change the world through prayer? Yes, if
enough of us use a magic power which is in all of us, and
use it to an avowed purpose of making this a better world
for all. What we truly want is to make all human life
more secure, happier, freer and more worth while. We
have the power within us to do just that!

I have watched this power at work in men, women, and

children from all walks of life. You yourself can trace its working through the history of mankind on earth, and I believe you will agree with me that it is the one power which has led man from his one-cell beginning to his present state.

This power is the only one which can hold our complicated civilization together. It is the only power which can save us from complete annihilation by the machines we have created and are now using to destroy the races of man and the natural resources of our earth.

We have this power for the using. There is nothing in all the universe that can force us to make use of it. But if we reject it, then almost certainly a force which is its negative and opposite takes its place and rules our lives. This negative force is nothing in itself, but is as darkness is to light.

I watched a woman use this magic power to climb from the pitiful status of derelict and charity patient to a happy marriage, a home of her own, a useful life, and more money than she knows what to do with. I watched another woman refuse this power and let its dark opposite work through her, driving her husband and son away from her forever, and bringing on her own death in an asylum.

Young people have used it to overcome fear of the grown-up and wiser world around them. Through it they found happiness and a life-path open invitingly before them.

Men have discovered and used this power to build careers and fortunes, for through it they learned how to handle every problem that arose. Others have used it to save and rebuild old fortunes, hold homes and businesses together. I have seen it open prison doors and lift people out of sick beds.

What *is* this wonder working power? Why *love,* of course!

Love is the greatest constructive power and the greatest healing agency and the widest gate to wisdom in all the universe. Hate is love's dark opposite.

And what is love? Love is caring about something with all the fervor of which the heart is capable. Love is a whole of many parts which include all we know of gratitude, appreciation, hope, trust, tolerance, patience, kindness, goodness, mercy, liberty, freedom, and justice. Love is the whole of everything we know to be good in the furthering and protecting of life and in pursuing final truth, beauty, and wisdom. God is love.

Love can heal alike the problems of the individual and of the nations. Instinctively we know this to be true. We value love above wisdom and above life itself. And rightly so. For without love life could not be maintained on earth, neither by the individual nor by the group. No individual life would be safe an hour. Without love, there could be no successful program of reproduction of the species, for without love there would be no care of the young, no learning, no civilization, no people on earth.

Through love God created man and brought him thus far on his way. When man was a mere tadpole in the warm oceans the three urges to live, love and grow were at work in him. Those little "creatures" loved their lives enough to struggle to save them, and by that struggle learned and grew—forward. They produced after their kind and passed on their stored wisdom to their offspring. They maintained their lives in a changing world by a wisdom which we now call law of adaptation. The species who learned and adapted lived. Through every change of form man has been led onward through love. God never has let man fail. But having brought him to the point of free will, man is free to choose, and when he chooses outside the laws of love, he always chooses wrong. Suffering is the result.

Love has always been at work in the hearts of at least some men. We can look down the whole march of civilization and see this power of love at work. Love of human beings and love of justice have produced among other things, life insurance, courts of law, policemen, safety and fire laws, food and health laws, child-protection laws, the right to vote, hospitals, and organized charity.

Love of wisdom has given rise to our philosophy, religion, and science. Love of beauty has produced our arts. Love is the very base of our civilization. It led cave man to culture and slaves to freedom.

Every injustice on earth today can be traced to lack of love. It is not the machine age which threatens civilization and our social order. The machine is one of man's greatest blessings, freeing his physical body and his objective mind, that he may have more leisure for learning and finding God.

We talk about keeping world peace by keeping the world fed, clothed, and housed. We do not need more ingenious ways of making two stalks of corn grow where one grew formerly; we need more brotherly love that teaches men how to help each other. We have this senseless circle: men devoting their lives and fortunes to research, wresting facts from nature, finding new ways to produce more food. This is prayer; and the prayer is answered. Then the new abundance of food is destroyed while millions on earth go hungry.

We do not need better institutions of learning as much as we need to teach brotherly love in the ones we have, so that no educated man becomes anti-social and uses his education and wits to rob and steal from his fellow men. We do not need more laws prohibiting the actions and freedom of the individual in order to bring about a better social order with more peace and prosperity for all. Quite the opposite. We need more freedom, but there can not be more freedom until we have more brotherly love. If we had *enough* love we could wipe half the laws off the statute books and be the better for it. When men learn to conduct themselves uprightly through love of good instead of through fear of punishment, we will have complete freedom.

The eye for an eye and a tooth for a tooth philosophy that remembers old hurts for generations and demands payment in kind is a wrong conception of the universal law of cause and effect. But Jesus came to give the world a new law, a law which supersedes the old one; the law of love and forgiveness.

There is but one question before the world: Shall we accept the teachings of Jesus Christ as a way of life for all, or shall we deny them and follow each man his own rule and way?

In John 3:16 Jesus tells us why He came to earth. He says "For God so loved the world, that he gave his only begotten Son that whosoever believeth in him should not perish, but have everlasting life."

Jesus' whole ministry was one of love. By His parables and His own acts, He gave humanity the pattern for individual and world peace and salvation. If we accept the Christian doctrine as a way of life for all and conduct ourselves accordingly, we can change our lives and our world through prayer. For if we accept Christ we must accept His doctrine of brotherly love. We must obey His command that "Ye love one another; as I have loved you." If we faithfully practice brotherly love we shall find that we are living by prayer.

And what if we do *not* accept Christ?

In our economic world we have denied Christ and we see poverty amidst plenty, millions hungry on the one hand while food is destroyed on the other to keep prices high. We see men naked and cold, while we plow under cotton.

We have denied Christ in our industrial world and we have problems of labor and capital, strikes, fights, turmoil, and strife, and the end is not yet.

We have denied Christ in our relations to our fellow men and we have race hatreds. We have minority group problems. We have denied Him and we have wars which murder our people and devastate our earth and create problems for generations to come.

In our private lives and hearts we have denied Christ and we see divorce, crime, and child delinquency at an all time high.

We have denied Christ in our ideology and we have brother fighting against brother. We have professions banding together to benefit themselves at the expense of the people. We have unions and associations and lobbys set up for a private gain at a public loss.

After God had brought us on our way as far as we could come by blind nature or instinct, He gave us free will. That is where we are like Him. But man, having free will, decided to use it, and to no longer look to God alone and to be led by Him. Is not this the real meaning in the story of Adam and Eve and the fall of man? Man set out to live alone, and was soon in trouble. The troubles multiplied and finally man, never being able completely to lose sight of God, decided to look to Him again. The old Testament of the Bible tells us of this search for One who would lead them back to God, and to everlasting life. The old prophets foretold the coming of Christ.

And "God so loved the world that he gave—" through Christ, the answer to every problem we shall ever face, either as an individual, a nation or a world. "Love ye one another, even as I have loved you."

Not millions of dollars, not elaborate plans and boards

and departments, armies and navies and taxes. No, that is not what we need to change the world, to give it permanent, lasting peace. Love—that is all we need.

Not money, but love is what makes the world go round. Remove love from the hearts of every person in America and it would not only go bankrupt in a week, but every hall of learning would close, along with every church and institution of mercy, justice, and protection of life and property. Money is of no value without love. What good are books and teachers if one does not love wisdom? What good are courts, if one does not love justice? Where there is no love there is no life, no truth, no beauty, no wisdom worth the having. To have life without love, one might as well be a vegetable or a microbe.

Someone may say, oh, yes, the world does need love, but what can I do? I am but one. My friend, nothing worth while in the world ever has been done except by individuals. Sometimes they band together. Would you like to help heaven come to earth? Then like Abou Ben Adhem be one who loves your fellow men! Look upon their worried faces, their tired sick bodies. Hear their cries. Consider the problems in the land. Out of many select but one, or only one phase of one problem which today torments humanity, and work in that little corner. Work at it with all the fervor of which your heart is capable. Lose your life and find your soul. Oh, feed His sheep!

Don't think you can't serve humanity through the power of love. Every great reform, every great service of mercy, has grown out of the love of some individual's heart.

Florence Nightingale loved humanity. She dared to break the set custom of her day to go forth and nurse men—the war wounded. Elizabeth Fry, spurred by the love in her heart, made it her business to help poor prisoners of England. She went to Newgate Prison and, shocked at what she learned, what others accepted as right or beyond cure, she began her reforms which spread over Europe. No prison has been quite so bad since.

The Red Cross grew out of love and is maintained by it. Love of music spurred a piano teacher from Missouri to work for "music under the stars" for all and today we can thank Mrs. Artie Carter for Hollywood Bowl. And up in Chicago, a determined woman who had no money but a great deal of love for babies whose parents could not or did not want to take care of them, and for people who wanted to be parents but had no babies, got the financial help she needed and The Cradle was born.

We can count it as law that no endeavor born of love ever will fail. No love ever was lost. Our churches, our hospitals, our institutions of learning with their underpaid and hard-working servants unto Him, never could have survived but for the power of love.

Look around you, select a problem, put love to work, take God as your partner in your plan to serve your fellow men, and you cannot fail. And you will find such peace and joy as you do not now dream exists.

Do you truly want to change your life through prayer? Would you like to help make the world a better place for all? Do you want people to love you? Do you want some one individual to love you just for yourself alone? Then learn to love, learn to pray without ceasing. If you are unmarried, longing for love and a mate, then do not look for someone to love you, but seek with diligence for someone to love. Love goes where it is welcomed. When the very air around you becomes impregnated with your love for others, when everyone you know realizes that you love the best in them, then love will come to you, for nothing can or wants to keep it away.

In Emerson's essay on *Compensation* he says: "Love, and you shall be loved. All love is mathematically just, as much as the two sides of an algebraic equation." When one comes along who appreciates all that is highest and best in us and, like God, forgives the worst in us and invites us to sit by the fire of his own great good love, thus restoring our faith in ourselves, how can we turn away from such a one! We cannot. We love him.

In working with people who have been convicted of crimes I find that they never blame themselves for their acts. Every man at least glimpses the kind of man he could be if he would follow the dictates of his soul. He does not want to be judged as a final and finished character on the evidence of his acts alone. We all know there always is more to us than appears on the surface. The criminal makes excuses for his outer act, stoutly maintaining that he "is not a criminal at heart." Nor is he. And I have never met one whose life would not have been different, had he had love at the time and in the way he needed it.

When we learn to love even a fraction as much as Jesus loved, we shall know how to handle every human relation problem with ease. He said to the sinning woman, "Neither do I condemn thee," and did not ask punishment or put a brand of shame upon the poor creature. His only admonition was to "sin no more." He told the thief on the cross with him, "Today shalt thou be with me in paradise." And He cried out, "Father, forgive them; for they know not what they do," on behalf of His persecutors. Oh, could *we* but love and forgive our fellow men as Christ Jesus asked us to do! Could we but forgive seventy times seven. Could we but see past the sin, the mistake, to the man's soul, to his likeness to God and, forgetting the bad, love the good in him. Dare we try to follow in His steps? Only to the extent that we do will we change our lives and our world from what they are to what we want them to be.

Bible students and teachers of metaphysics see deep

and hidden meanings in every one of Jesus' words. They say that modern science, especially in the field of physics, is rapidly proving every claim that Jesus made concerning the kingdom of heaven. For example, they say that Jesus knew all about space-time and relativity as evidenced in His seeing the harvest which those around could not see and said was months away. But you and I need not concern ourselves with these deep matters. We can obey Jesus, use that child-like approach and find Him. We need not ask whether Christian principles will work in the world for all. We can see and test for ourselves His teachings concerning love.

Jesus told us to love children. Now we realize that love is the most important treasure we can give our children. Baby specialists are telling us that the young child simply must be made aware of its parents' love, if it is to thrive as it should. A noted woman physician recently wrote a book about young babies withering and all but dying from no other cause than the lack of love.

To the growing child nothing is so important as the sense of security which love gives him. Not only love for the child by the parents but love between the parents. I have seen boisterous, ill-behaved children turned into models of deportment by being given a definite part of the family life and work which assured them they were needed and wanted. Every case of child delinquency can be charged up to the lack of love.

We have long thought of the importance of love to women. But business men tell me that a man cannot succeed in life if he has not the love of at least one good woman. If not a wife, then a mother, a sister, or a friend. And I have the word of an expert for it that the high rate of failure of men starting small individual business adventures lies not in their inability but in the lack of love.

People sometimes say, "If God loves us, why does He let thus and so happen?" It helps to compare God's love for us with the love of earthly parents for their children. Long before the child is born good parents have made plans for it, taking steps and precautions for its future welfare. They work for it, make ready for its arrival. They love and protect it with their very lives if need be, even when it is still so young that it is utterly unaware of its own existence or theirs.

As the child grows they teach him as rapidly as his developing intellect will permit. The parents hope that the child will some day develop far enough to recognize them and love them in return. But if, later, that child refuses the parental counsel and love, insists upon leaving home and living his own life, even though it may lead to unhappiness and poverty, good and wise parents will permit him to live his own life, knowing that it is his divine privilege to scorn their love, their advice, and even their desire to help

That is the picture of God and the human race, is it not? It seems that all our Creator ever brought us into existence for was to have something to love, something that would love Him in return, something on His equal plane. In order to do this, man had to have free will. To have created us so that we were forced to love our Creator, forced to do His will, would have robbed us of free will, the power of choosing, and, hence, defeated our Creator's primary purpose.

In all the history of man there is no evidence that God ever stopped loving man for one instant. Jesus knew this so well. He tried so hard and so patiently to tell us about our relation to God. Jesus called Him the Father, and said that all that the Father has is ours if we will but call on Him and ask that our daily needs be met. But there were certain rules which had to be followed. We are to forgive our debtors if we expect God to forgive our debts. That is the law of love at work. It is at work throughout the universe, for God is love.

Surely we know the Golden Rule is the law of love at work. Einstein is right, if but two per cent of the people lived by the law of love they could change the world and rule it by and through love.

Would you truly change your life through prayer? Then pray for love to rule your head and heart and hand.

Go into your closet. Be still. Say: *"Great Infinite Spirit, in me and around me, everywhere present, I thank thee for life, love, and wisdom. Work through me as You worked through Christ Jesus. Teach me to do thy will."*

Try this prayer for a month. Be sincere. Think deeply about it. Live up to it. When a problem arises ask yourself, "How would Jesus Christ have handled this problem?" and act accordingly.

If you will follow this program you will gradually find your work is becoming a prayer; that the morning is blessed to you, and that you can pray while you rest. Your eyes will be opened to good all around you that you did not notice before. You will meet new people to love and see new ways to serve. Friends will come unbidden. Your health and fortune will improve. Your mind will become keen and alert and new truths will become evident to you. Life will move in an orderly sequence of desire, work, fulfillment, and happiness.

Keep it up long enough and you will change your whole life for the better.

Oh, open your heart and let Him in! For he who will receive Christ and so use enough of God's life and love and wisdom, will also receive all the good that the universe has to offer in this world and in all the worlds to come.

CHAPTER ELEVEN

Keep a Record of Answered Prayer

This book was first published August 14, 1945, by Dodd, Mead & Company in a hard-cover edition. It went through twenty printings in the United States under the Dodd, Mead imprint, had some separate mail-order printings and was also published in England. Today it is widely read in Japan and is now being translated into Portuguese for Brazil and into Spanish for other South American countries.

Now it is June of 1971, and this book you have in your hand is the first edition in paperback, under a new publisher, DeVorss & Company. All the material in part four has been written especially for this new paperback edition.

Since 1945, I have had six other books published and am currently finishing book eight. Judging from letters through the years, I felt that many of my readers would like to know something of the story of this first book beyond what is covered in the preface and something of my life and times that followed, which resulted in those other six books.

Many people have written me saying that after a successful prayer project, "worse things happened than before," and asked what they could do about it. Others complained that it did little good to try to straighten out their own lives "when the world is in such a mess."

So, twenty-five years and six books later, I am happy to have this opportunity to try to help my readers a little further.

In order to prepare this material, I first read through each of the other six books and then read again, *Change Your Life Through Prayer.* I would not change one word of the original edition. But I do see more clearly than ever before the necessity of the set of twelve books that I hope to finish.

Next, I went through some of my files of case histories —records of people with problems and problem people I have worked with in prayer and teaching, the last quarter of a century. A few of the case histories given in my books have become famous. People have written to me from over the world wanting to know more about Jenny, whose story is told in my second book, *Change Your Life Through Love.* The greatest number of my case histories never have been presented. Together they cover just about every facet and phase of human problems. Every time I look into that file I am inspired anew on seeing the evidence of the power of prayer to change lives and conditions.

Through the years I have also received many letters asking me if I ever had any "real problems" in my own life. So I looked into my personal diary which I have kept off and on since 1934.

Some of my personal problems included a divorce, in 1936, from my first husband, Elmer Lloyd Terrill, a brilliant newspaper man, father of my two children, a girl and a boy. This brought with it all the attendant problems any mother alone with two young children faces. Times were not easy for anyone. Hitler was threatening Europe and in spite of the hopeful "Peace in Our Time" promised by the Four-Power peace pact signed with Hitler, his German troops invaded Poland in 1939 and World War Two began.

Then in 1940, for the first time in history, the United States Peace Time Draft was enacted and many mothers, including myself, felt that it was only a matter of time until our sons would be called to war. On December 7, 1941, Japan bombed Pearl Harbor. We were in World War Two up to our eyebrows.

In February, 1942, Herbert James Mann and I were married. He had a married son from a first marriage that had ended in divorce. Both his first wife and my first husband were still living.

If you think a second marriage in any house does not bring problems with it, take a look at current history around you. But if you think a second marriage never can be happy or successful, just read the account of the great happiness we found in our second marriage. Some of it is given in my book on overcoming fear; but more especially, my last book, *Beyond the Darkness*, published in 1965, tells of what happened to Herbert on March 14th, 1961, and his death April 19, following. This book lists some personal problems and tells something of our lives together those nineteen happy, wonderful, growing, fulfilling and sometimes wacky years. But its purpose is to report on the personal experiences which sent me on a journey of questions concerning what happens after death, and some of the answers I found.

The death of Herbert presented more questions to me about God, man and their relationship, the structure and purpose of the Christian religion, the reality of prayer and the destiny of man than anything else I ever had faced. I was forced to examine everything I had read, heard, and had previously been taught to believe. Out of all this came my solid conviction given in the last chapter, "Three Reasons Why I believe We Live After Death." Agreeing and doubting Christian Ministers and church members still write me about it.

There is no point in reciting personal problems that

came since 1934. There is a new one every day—almost every hour—with decisions to be made, action to be taken. But there is a big point in saying that I do not call these "happenings" problems. They are invitations to Soul growth. Every day is examination day to see how our Soul is progressing toward its ultimate goal of freedom; which proves the value of keeping a record of answered prayer.

After going over all seven books, case histories, my personal diary, there remained the task of checking my records of answered prayer.

I keep these records in hard-cover, three-ring loose leaf notebooks. Keeping a record of answered prayer is one of the "musts" for my students. They learn to refer to it when a new problem or opportunity arises. They early discover that such reviewing builds their faith. And as Jesus showed, faith is the key to all answered prayer.

Besides my personal record of answered prayer, I keep a sort of record of current history and public prayers. During the last thirty-six years there have been times when the whole civilized world got down on its knees—like the hell and the miracle of Dunkirk, for instance. Do you remember it?

Well, Hitler's armies had pushed the French and English soldiers by the tens of thousands, down into a trap, the small port town of Dunkirk, in France, with no possible means of escape except smack into the English Channel. Good people the world over sat by their radios and wept. You see, the German method to conquer the world was perfect. Hitler had one thousand scientists working for him. Those methodical Germans knew how many ounces of gold they had and even how many chamber pots. They had perfected a system of lies and brutality—*great gas ovens for the extermination of thousands of human beings*—concentration camps where people were treated as less than animals. They even "put to sleep" the old, helpless and children who were sick, or a drag to "the plan."

On May 26, 1940, the world learned that there was no escape for those trapped men. The big British ships could not move into that small port. Hitler was going to win! Millions began to pray. King George of England called for a time of prayer. Churches and private homes were filled with praying people.

The following morning the first part of the miracle was in evidence—some straggling little old boats—quaint, queer water craft, almost anything that would float, plus yachts of sportsmen, racing yawls, motor launches—manned by men without guns or uniforms but with love in their hearts and prayers in their souls and a trust in God, were streaming in from all over the British Isles. That hell of evacuating those men while the Germans strafed them from the sky, continued nine days and nights; and so did the prayers of the civilized world. A novena, you know, means nine days and nights of prayer. Records show that 338,226 lives were saved. The Germans hadn't counted on prayer-power. They were relying on fire-power. And Winston Churchill had found that "their finest hour" had been lived through by quite ordinary people who believed in God, prayer, honor, life, truth, beauty and freedom for the individual. Men who were willing to risk their own lives in an effort to save the lives and freedom of others.

But the war went on and grew worse by the day. When Japan bombed Pearl Harbor, millions began to pray anew. Most of them never had stopped praying. People who have proved the power of prayer turn to it when trouble comes.

The War of the Pacific was on and rationing of certain foods and gasoline followed. (I still have some of my unused stamps.) My son went off to take Merchant Marine training with the Navy. (He later served in the army also.) My daughter, after graduating from high school, did war work. Herbert, being an architect and engineer, got into war work stationed in Arizona. I continued writing, praying, keeping house, working with people in prayer, keeping open house on Sunday with dinner for strangers in uniform. Attending church on Sunday was a privilege for people. Young people had no time nor inclination for a "drug culture."

Then it was June 6, 1944—D-Day—the big Allied Invasion in Europe which had been planned since Dunkirk. The world stayed glued to its radio, praying without ceasing. Hitler was stopped. The war in Europe was over. Prayers continued. Families wanted their service men home, and the men wanted to come home; but the War in the Pacific continued.

One of my answered prayers of those days had to do with my wanting to attend the Peace Conference in San Francisco, in 1945. Neither love nor money could get you in. You had to have business there, and a card. The card was granted by mail and I went up to San Francisco only to learn that the "officials," had lost my card and rating. I was not allowed to cross the "deadline." An armed Marine stood guard to see that neither I, nor anyone else crossed without that card of admission. For a few days I stayed in Palo Alto with Herbert's Sister and her Scientist husband, Dr. Herman A. Spoehr until, card cleared, I would be guaranteed a room in San Francisco. One night I slept on a cot in a clothes closet in the hotel where my cousin Bertha Schellenger lived. People from all over the world filled the city to the Bay. Through Prayer (and some pestering, I admit) I finally got that needed card and was assigned to a hotel room with a most interesting woman who was an official interpreter at the Conference.

The world was afire with hope over that first Peace Conference, later called United Nations. I could *feel* the prayers and hopes of the peoples of the world who wanted permanent peace; but human selfishness, national pride, greed, individual interests were glaringly present.

Then it was the day of August 14, 1945. My husband and I, who were living in Santa Monica at the time, were listening to the radio message of President Truman telling of the Bomb, Hiroshima, the Japanese surrender, and that peace—when the door bell rang.

Herbert answered it and brought in a brown cardboard box the postman had just delivered.

"It is the copies of your new book," Herbert said, noting the sticker on the box.

I had known for months that August 14 was the publication date, but had forgotten it. "Oh put it down," I said. "We can open it later. We are listening to history!"

But Herbert went on calmly opening the box, though visibly excited. When he reached in and lifted out one of the copies showing Durer's famius Praying Hands on the jacket front, he just stood there a moment, silent. Then he said, with tears in his voice, *"Change Your Life Through Prayer!"* making it sound like a command with a flourish of trumpets.

Swallowing my own tears, I reached for the book he handed me.

"Here is the answer for tomorrow's world without war," Herbert said solemnly, gently, in that wonderful way he had of speaking. "We never can build a better world without first building better people."

Then he kissed me, and held me in his arms a moment. We were thinking of friends, relatives, still in the war; of my brother's son who had visited us before going off to war in Europe and being killed there. He had wanted to become a doctor. We were thinking of the world of peace, music, truth, beauty, love and laughter and freedom for every man, that our hearts so much desired and for which we daily prayed, and wondering what great new good the years of peace would bring.

And so the life of this book began. I started to lecture on the book in November of that year and am still lecturing on my books.

Looking back, it is evident that the last quarter of a century has been more thrilling, rapidly moving—at once more shocking, horrifying and glorifying—than any other twenty-five years of recorded history. That is because more people were involved at the same time in world-wide events than ever before. Also, the development of rapid transportation, communication through television and radio, mass production of everything from food to reading materials has made it possible for millions of people, for the first time in history, to learn what is going on around the world.

Not everyone knew how to evaluate these fast-moving events. Many did not want to learn so much as to be entertained or distracted. But everything witnessed—the sorrows and the joys, the ugliness and the beauty, *became a part of the subconscious mind* of billions of people.

A few of the things witnessed by millions were:

The assassination of John F. Kennedy, the 35th President of the United States, and the landing on the moon of two Americans: Neil Armstrong and Edwin Aldrin; the condition of millions of illiterates trying self-rule; riots, campus "unrest," sing-ins and walk outs. They heard Bishop Pike declare he had communicated with his deceased son "on the other side."

They have seen and heard the news of Vietnam, draft cards being burned, and "peace marches." They've been told that the Socialist state has failed in Australia and England and that in the United States the Welfare load, plus the continued demands of labor unions, threaten to wreck the United States economy. They've learned that people are leaving churches that are supporting the Black Panthers; that juvenile crime is at an all-time high. And they've been able to read some of the best books ever published. Many have now read the famous twenty-five books that changed American history.

The great, good, truth is, that every individual who witnessed the events of the past twenty-five years was forced to take sides and to admit to himself, "I am *for* that," or "I am *against* that." All of which adds up to the fact that the world will never again be the same. *It will be better!* Because new millions have seen a better way of life and have decided they will work for that better way.

One of the most heartening facts of the past twenty-five years has been the new, scientific approach to the power of prayer. Space here does not permit listing any of the hundreds of reports, studies, examples, etc., by so-called "cold science." The good news is that prayer is being studied, used, relied upon by more people than ever before in the history of the world. We are at last beginning to understand what Jesus was talking about when he said prayer could move mountains, and why and how the answer to prayer does depend upon faith.

I believe that by the year 2000 science will have proved so much about the creative power of prayer and the spiritual laws under which this power operates, that it will usher in a religious renaissance that will sweep and uplift the whole world. If enough people would keep a record of their answered prayers and make a habit of reviewing them often, they would help to change the spiritual atmosphere of the world for the better. We now know that every thought, feeling, desire, intention of fear or faith, love or hate, goes out from the individual and creates an atmosphere "after its kind." It is a law of nature and one we can depend upon.

These days, we are hearing a great deal about the dangers of pollution of our physical-material world. But the greater danger is in the pollution of our Spiritual atmosphere. Millions are now remembering that it was the *immoral atmosphere* which infected the mighty Roman Empire that brought on the evils which caused her fall. Many people think the United States of America will fall for the same reason. But I do not agree. Millions who have learned how to work with the power of prayer are busy with our world-wide prayer project.

The answer to the two questions before mentioned: why do bad things happen after prayer has been answered; and why should we keep a record of answered prayer, is this:

To receive an answer to prayer is to be lifted up to a higher level of consciousness. If we forget it, are ungrateful, we sink back to a lower level of consciousness and are likely to bring a "worse thing" upon ourselves in an unconscious desire for punishment to make amends and set the record straight.

Now, to keep a record of answered prayers, and pray for and with others, has the effect of *building the consciousness* of the one who prays. He can go through, as the 91st Psalm tells us, no matter what is happening to the rest of the world at the time. He can keep the good he has obtained through prayer.

Dr. Alexix Carrell said of prayer: "It is the only power in the world that seems to overcome the so-called laws of nature."

Since this is true, why don't we use this power more often for ourselves and others? In my years of working with people I have found that many who desire a better life and a better world never get started on a prayer program because they lack a method of procedure.

In the next chapter I will explain something of the method I use and teach.

CHAPTER TWELVE

Pray For and With Others

We are interested in holding and multiplying the good
we gain through prayer. There is no other way to build
a better world for ourselves and for all people. Keeping a report on answered prayer increases our *individual
faith*. To pray for others helps to increase the *faith of
the world*. That is back of the great good of public prayers.
The safer the whole world becomes, the happier and safer
the individual will be.

The Bible tells us about the potential powers of man.
But we need a method of procedure that will enable us
to develop these powers for everday use and Soul growth.
Jesus spells out the method in the power of prayer, but the
points are not given in neat numerical order. To use prayer
power in right sequence we first must read, compare, understand and prove for ourselves by use, the points found.
Trying to find and get these points together in working
sequence is what I have been working on all these years.

It is imposible to report on the full amount of work
done through the years. I have continued to study, attend
classes, work with private teachers and of course, I learn
from the classes I conduct and the prayer groups I work
with. Here we have space only to report briefly something of the method worked out.

Prayer is a power. All power is locked in law. Prayer
power like that of electricity, travels in a circle. That is
why it is "done unto you as you believe." Prayer produces
after the pattern set.

There are two kinds of prayer: under Grace, and under Law. Jesus used both but taught the way of law which anyone can learn and use at will while perfecting his Soul to the point of Christ-Consciousness faith. My experience with prayers under Grace is that they require great emotion, as in a life and death matter. Instant answers come under that method. Prayers under law require knowledge, self-discipline, patience and a conscious keeping of the total law.

There are twelve points of the spiritual laws which flow down from the principle of prayer. Why this is the method we should learn and daily use is explained in my six books which followed this one.

In Mark 11:24 Jesus tells us what happens when we pray correctly. His whole teaching tells us how to keep from ruining our faith in the believe-receive law. His two great Commandments—love God, neighbor and self—are the key to keeping our faith because every time we go contrary to the law of love we damage our faith to some degree.

My continued efforts in learning the laws and how best to present them resulted in those six books. Here, we can only mention them by title and purpose. To the person who desires to live a happy, successful and meaningful life, I respectfully suggest that he obtain and study them in the order in which they were written, as follows:

Book 1. *Change Your Life Through Prayer*
We must meet the law of asking. "Ask, seek, knock," and we find.

Book 2. *Change Your Life Through Love*
Love is the key to generating and holding faith. "Those who love know God." And, "God is love."

Book 3. *Change Your Life Through Faith and Work*
"Faith without works is dead." And work without faith

is buried in drudgery, resentment and lack of joyous living.

Book 4. *How To Use The Power Of Your Word.*

We are both justified and condemned by our word. "Both life and death are in the power of the tongue." Jesus had to "speak the word only," for the Centurion's servant to be healed.

Book 5. *How To Live In The Circle Of Prayer And Make Your Dreams Come True.*

This book is the key to my teaching and contains the twelve points of creative prayer as I have worked them out and used them with my private students for years. I created the circle of prayer chart which you will find on page 164.

This book, first published by Dodd, Mead & Co. in 1959, was repossessed and I sold it to the Unity School of Christianity. It was then run as a serial in the illustrated magazine *New* and has now been published by *Unity* in hard cover under the title: *Make Your Dreams Come True.* This is the title I generally use when I lecture for industry, business and professional groups. It is the same book, word for word as originally published. It contains the circle chart. Only the title has been accented differently, using the last clause first.

Book 6. *How To Analyze and Overcome Your Fears.*

As far back as Job it was known that "what I feared came upon me and what I greatly feared was done unto unto me." Fear arises as a result of one or more of the four false beliefs about God and man and their relationship. Job's wrong conception of God let him in for fears that became realities in his life.

Book 7. *Beyond the Darkness.*

This book I had not planned to write. I did plan to do a book about prayers, rest, meditation, etc., and the questions of life after death, reincarnation and how our ideas on these points of life affect our daily living. But as mentioned, after the events that led to the death of my husband and those that followed, I felt I had to write the book to help those who needed answers now.

We need to know those twelve rules in order to safely pray for ourselves or others. In my prayer groups where each one prays for and with others, such prayers as "And, Dear God, please see that Jane marries George," are common. My students are instructed that such a prayer is tinkering with the free will of others and is therefore breaking the law of love.

There is such a thing as using prayer for evil purposes which the world long has known and called black magic. It can be used by strong minds over weak, by informed minds over ignorant and innocent and fearful minds. I have a case history in the Circle Dream book (No. 5) which shows the tragedy of such use of prayer. The Communists have learned a great deal about "brain washing," and "sleep teaching," and "getting lies believed," and criminal psychology. But they apparently have not yet learned that there is a universal higher law than that lower one. The higher law warns us never to use the power of creative prayer except under the law of love with a desire for good for all and harm for none. The scientists among the Communists are rising higher and higher in consciousness. They will eventually "discover" God. And the whole plan of Communism will be seen for what it is, and given up.

To sum it up:

To keep a record of answered prayer and to review it often, builds our faith and helps us to hold the good we have obtained through prayer.

We pray for and with others because "where two are agreed" it greatly increases the power. I don't know why, but I do know that this is so. Some of my prayer groups have generated faith and love and such high expectancy that we could "feel the presence of the Spirit." Early Christians often experienced this and it could come for a whole world at prayer. This is what Jesus promised— to be in the midst of praying people. Think back over your own experiences in time of great world stress or danger when millions were praying. Didn't you feel that "something" hovering over the earth? There are many records of this "something" during World War One. It was true during the earthquake here in Southern California on Feb. 9th, this year. Some day, we will have truly a world at prayer, and a higher civilization and greater happiness for the individual than the world now dreams of. Reason enough, surely, for all of us to keep on trying.

—end—

CIRCLE OF PRAYER

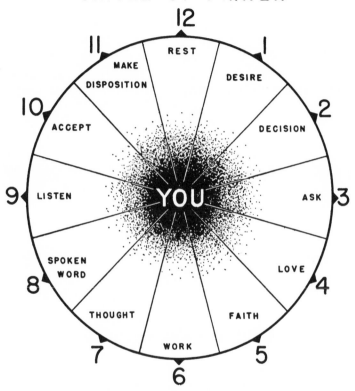

The complete interpretation of this chart, and how to use it, will be found in my book *Make Your Dreams Come True.*

The Story of Praying Hands

THOUSANDS OF ART LOVERS own copies of Albrecht
Dürer's *Praying Hands,* which is reproduced on the
jacket of this book. Perhaps hundreds of thousands have
seen it on Church programs for it is widely used, being
the most celebrated of all the great artist's paintings.
There is a statue of it in a small chapel at Northwestern
University. It is to be found in practically every art
store in the civilized world. And yet few people know
the heart-warming story behind it.

When this book was first published, in August, 1945,
I began to receive inquiries about "those hands," on the
cover. I still am receiving them. Every time I lecture
someone asks me about "those expressive" or "those
fascinating and haunting" hands. So my publishers have
asked me to retell the story of *Praying Hands,* and here
it is, a compilation from many sources.

Along about 1490, Albrecht Dürer and a young man
known now only as Hans, were struggling artist friends.
Some sources place them in France, others in Austria
and still others in Germany. In any case they were very
poor and had to work to support themselves while they
studied. Work kept them from classes. Progress was
slow. Then one day Hans, the older of the two, insisted
that Albrecht devote all his time to study while he, Hans,
worked to support them both. They agreed that when
Albrecht was successful he would in turn support Hans
who would then learn to paint.

The bargain was struck. Albrecht went off to the

cities of Europe to study painting. His was more than talent. It was genius, as the world now knows. He was soon successful and went back to keep his bargain with Hans. But Albrecht quickly discovered the price his devoted friend had paid. For Hans had worked at manual labor, hard rough work, in order to support his friend. His slender, sensitive artist's hands had been ruined for life. Those stiff, gnarled fingers could no longer use the artist's brush in the sure and delicate strokes necessary to painting. So Albrecht Dürer, great artist and great soul, painted the hands of his friend, painted them as he had so often seen them raised in prayer for their success. It is said he presented this painting to Hans.

Today, art galleries throughout the civilized world still have exhibitions of Albrecht Dürer's paintings and etchings. But of them all, beautiful and famous as they are, none holds the place in the hearts of the people as does *Praying Hands,* which tells its own eloquent story of love and labor and sacrifice on the part of the subject, and of love and gratitude of the painter.

Since I believe all honest work is prayer, I was very happy when my publishers decided to use *Praying Hands* on the cover of my book. I hope the story behind it will add to your pleasure in reading the book.

Sincerely,

STELLA TERRILL MANN

Pasadena, May, 1949.